THE
INSTANT POT®
KOSHER
COOKBOOK

THE
INSTANT POT®
— KOSHER —
COOKBOOK

100 RECIPES TO
NOURISH BODY AND SOUL

PAULA SHOYER

STERLING EPICURE
New York

STERLING EPICURE
New York

An Imprint of Sterling Publishing Co., Inc.
122 Fifth Avenue
New York, NY 10011

ISBN 978-1-4549-3753-1
ISBN 978-1-4549-3754-8 (e-book)

Distributed in Canada by Sterling Publishing Co., Inc.
c/o Canadian Manda Group, 664 Annette Street
Toronto, Ontario M6S 2C8, Canada
Distributed in the United Kingdom by GMC Distribution Services
Castle Place, 166 High Street, Lewes, East Sussex BN7 1XU, England
Distributed in Australia by NewSouth Books
University of New South Wales, Sydney, NSW 2052, Australia

For information about custom editions, special sales, and premium and corporate purchases,
please contact Sterling Special Sales at 800-805-5489 or specialsales@sterlingpublishing.com.

Manufactured in Malaysia

2 4 6 8 10 9 7 5 3 1

sterlingpublishing.com

Cover design by David Ter-Avanesyan and Elizabeth Mihaltse Lindy
Interior design by Shannon Nicole Plunkett

Photo credits on page 204

For my husband Andy, daughter Emily, and
sons Sam, Jake, and Joey, the best cheerleaders
around, I love you for always making me
feel that I can do anything

CONTENTS

VEGETARIAN MAINS — 123

SIDE DISHES — 145

DESSERTS — 173

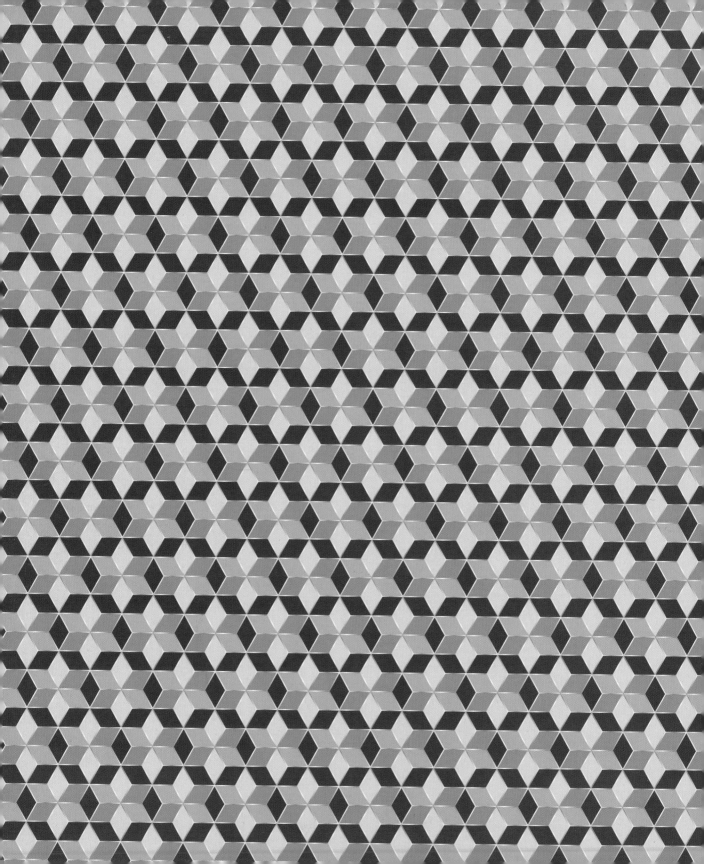

COOKING WITH YOUR INSTANT POT®

PEOPLE HAVE TOLD ME I AM GOOD UNDER PRESSURE, so it is surprising that I arrived on the Instant Pot® (IP) scene a bit late. Since 2017, people have been asking me for Instant Pot® versions of my recipes. I was busy with other projects and resisted acquiring yet another device to add to my cluttered kitchen.

After I had my IP® for only a few months, and already started raving about it, I learned about the Kosher Instant Pot® Facebook group, now with over 12,700 members. I spent a day reading through the posts and discussions and decided that this enthusiastic, committed, and supportive group needed a cookbook. First, I needed to become an expert myself, so I dove in and began using it all the time.

Instant Pot® Cooking Is the New Fast Food for Kosher People

The IP® is the hottest kitchen tool in decades, and it is quickly changing how people of all ages cook. Just like the microwave in the late 1960s and 1970s, the IP® is truly revolutionary. It is helping a gadget-savvy generation of college kids and young working adults cook more at home with fewer baking pans and tools—and has given mothers the ability to quickly feed growing families. In fact, the IP® is ideal for anyone who wants food fast with less cleanup.

It was clear to me, from the first IP® recipe I developed, that this device was perfect for the kosher cook and the Jewish home.

Jewish people do a really crazy amount of cooking—and not just for holidays. Our community is made up of working people who want to avoid the cost and calories of takeout, kosher college kids living off campus who miss homemade food, and parents of all ages with large families who need easy ways to feed their kids.

Jewish people basically cook Thanksgiving dinner every week for Shabbat. They need shortcuts and are tired of the traditional ways to make meals faster: sauces that are saturated with sugar and salt, grain side dishes out of a box, and other processed ingredients that reduce cooking prep steps.

Jewish food and the IP® are a natural fit. So many of our traditional dishes, whether from

Eastern Europe or North Africa, whether Persian or Mediterranean, are soups and stews—the sweet spot of the Instant Pot®. Historically, the dishes that defined our cuisine were literally composed of whatever we could find and afford, and then thrown into a pot and cooked for hours. Jews in Poland used to bring their pots of stews to the local bakery on Fridays to stay warm until lunch the next day. For decades, Jewish cooks have relied on slow cookers to achieve the soft, flavor-filled stews of their ancestors but lament the cooking time required. So many of those recipes were developed by women who didn't hold down full-time jobs outside the home. Today we want those traditional flavors but struggle to fit their creation into our busy lives. With the IP®, recipes that used to take hours are now ready in a fraction of the time.

The IP® is perfect for those really big holidays or when you are hosting a crowd, when you already have every burner going and three more pots waiting to take their turn. Now I can check off items on my cooking to-do list much faster, with equally fast cleanup in between.

Now "fast food" finally means something positive and nourishing.

Why Everyone Would Love to Have an Instant Pot®

It's fast. You can even place frozen meat or fish inside an Instant Pot®.

Easier cleanup. The whole dish is made, with few exceptions, in one metal bowl. Because you are adding many ingredients at the same time,

there are no piles and piles of bowls of ingredients to add at different stages. If you compare cleaning the IP® inner pot to a stovetop, there is no contest—today's fancy stovetops have many grooves that collect spilled sauces and are difficult to clean.

Less cooking effort. Once you've added all the ingredients to the pot, secured the lid, and pressed the buttons, you can simply go and do something else. There is no standing over a pot and checking on the dish over and over until the cooking time is done. This is especially helpful if you have small kids or aging parents around, and they actually need your attention. *It is much easier to master the IP® than you think.*

More nutritious. All of the nutrients and flavor stay inside the pot, and the speed allows food to retain more vitamins.

Kitchen stays cooler and smells stay inside. Consider a hot summer day when you are cooking for Shabbat, and all your burners and ovens are on. Even with the air-conditioning on high, your kitchen gets hot. The IP® gives off no heat, so you will use less air-conditioning to cool your kitchen. We all love those delicious smells coming from the kitchen when we bake challah or cookies or have chicken soup simmering for hours. But some recipes truly smell up your entire house—and not in a good way.

Use less energy and less water. The IP® is good for the environment because it uses less time and energy and fewer natural resources. And you no longer have to use as much water to cook rice or pasta.

Important Safety Rules

Today pressure cookers are safe and extremely easy to use. Your IP® comes with an instruction booklet that should be read and followed. The Instant Pot® is not a complicated device, despite all the buttons. I spent nine months writing this book and used it six days a week, and I did not use half of the buttons. After three recipes, you will be an expert. After five recipes, you will start adapting your own family favorites for the IP®. Be sure to follow these basic rules:

- Fill the pot no more than two-thirds full. There is a line in the inner pot to remind you of this.

- No deep frying in the pot.

- Follow the recipe precisely—I say this all the time, but seriously, **FOLLOW THE RECIPE.**

- Stay away from the steam while the IP® is venting.

- Use an aluminum foil sling (see below), silicone or other mitts, or a dishtowel to lift things out of the pot.

Insider Information

I love the Sauté function on the pot to brown aromatics, chicken, or meat before adding liquids and pressure-cooking. The mess stays inside rather than splattering all over your cookbook and stovetop, and best of all, the Sauté function helps add deep flavors to your dishes.

Deglazing the pan. After you sauté anything, before you add the next recipe ingredients, add some liquid to the pan and use a wooden spoon to scrape anything that may be stuck to the bottom of the pot. This step is critical to avoid the dreaded burn notice.

Pot-in-pot cooking. When you cook or bake something in a pan that goes inside your pot, on the steam rack, or over water, that's called pot-in-pot cooking. (Think of things you have traditionally baked in a water bath, such as meatloaf or cheesecake.) Pot-in-pot cooking—a method I use a lot—is also a great for making rice, kugel, cake, and so much more. You can insert and remove your pan of food by using an aluminum foil sling (see below).

Aluminum foil sling. This is a great hack, invented by Instant Pot® cooks before me, that helps you lift pans into and out of the inner pot when you do pot-in-pot cooking. Tear a piece of aluminum foil, about 20 inches (51cm) long, and place it on your counter. If you have heavy-duty foil, use that, and if not, use regular foil. Fold it in thirds the long way and flatten it with your hands. When you are ready to insert your pan into the pot, after you have added the water and steam rack into the inner pot, place the pan in the center of the foil and use the sides to lift and place it inside the pot on top of the rack. Fold the sides of the foil toward the center of the pan. When cooking is complete, you can use the ends of the sling to lift the pan out of the pot.

Thickening sauces and stews. This can be done either by cooking down the liquid by using the Sauté function, or by adding some cornstarch or flour. I scoop some of the liquid into a bowl, add the cornstarch or flour and mix in, and then return it to the pot to cook for a few more minutes.

Browning finished dishes. A quick visit to the oven broiler can give your dish the look of an oven-baked one.

Adapting recipes. If you want to adapt recipes that you love to make for cooking in the IP®, add more of the spices and sometimes more liquid to make sure the food doesn't stick to the bottom. Dishes with tomato sauce always need extra liquid.

The dreaded burn notice. From time to time, when I was developing recipes for this book, the display would read "burn" when the IP® was coming to pressure, which meant that food was stuck to the bottom of the pot and was burning. I would have to do a quick release of pressure, open the lid, and use a wooden spoon to scrape the bottom clean. I'd then add more liquid. If

you have to do this, reset the cooking time for a shorter period—by about 20 percent—than originally planned. Next time add more water.

You forgot to add an ingredient. Until the IP® comes to pressure and the float valve pops up, it is safe to open the lid and add an ingredient.

Instant Pot® Features

What size to purchase. I have 6-quart and 8-quart pots that I use for meat, and I love the larger 8-quart size for stock. All of the recipes in this book were tested in the 6-quart model. You can add one-third more of the ingredients in a recipe to cook in the 8-quart. The 8-quart takes longer to come to pressure. For meat dishes, you can add 25 percent more meat without changing the amount of liquid. Recipes in the 8-quart need at least 2 cups (500ml) of liquid, compared to the 1 cup (236ml) needed in the 6-quart.

Inner pot—the inner metal bowl that fits inside the device.

Float valve—the pin that goes up when the pressure has been achieved and drops when the pressure has been released.

Steam rack—the metal trivet that comes with the device. You can place food to cook on top of it with liquid below or use it for the pot-in-pot cooking method.

Steam release handle—the knob you turn to Sealing when you are cooking, and turn to Venting to release the pressure. On some models the steam release function is a lever, and on others it is a button that you push to release the pressure.

Lid—the cover of the pot that you lock in place before cooking.

Silicone ring—the ring inside the lid; should be replaced every 12 months or so, as it absorbs odors over time. To reduce odors, store an open box of baking soda in the device between uses.

How to Work the Display Panel

The panel has many buttons to use for cooking different types of food, and your instruction booklet explains how to use each cooking program option.

I typically use the manual feature by pressing the Pressure Cook button and setting the cooking time I want. Many people like the Rice button feature (see pages 146 and 147 for instructions). The recipes in this book always indicate which buttons to use. If they just state to pressure-cook for a specific number of minutes, just press Pressure and set the cooking time.

Steam. This feature is great for poaching fish.

Sauté. To sauté, press Sauté. When the display reads "Hot," add the oil or food to the inner pot. It usually takes 3 to 4 minutes for the pot to heat. You can adjust the level of the sauté heat by pressing the Sauté button until the desired level lights up on the display panel as low, medium, or high. Unless a recipe states otherwise, use the high level.

Pressure. Use this feature when you want to manually set the cooking time. Please note that the amount of time you set the IP® to pressure-cook is not the total cooking time. The device needs time to come to pressure, which could be as little as 5 minutes or as much as 25 minutes. The recipes in this book indicate the approximate time it takes for the IP® to come to pressure, so you can plan accordingly. You can press the Pressure button to adjust to low and high pressure. All of the recipes in this book use high pressure.

Warm. After the cooking time is done, the device automatically shifts to Warm—if the Auto Keep Warm button is on—and the panel will indicate how many minutes your dish has been warming. The warm feature can be used for 10 hours.

Slow Cook. I use this feature to keep food warm for Shabbat lunch.

Cancel. Press Cancel after the cooking time is achieved, unless you want your dish to remain on Warm, which the device shifts to automatically if the Warm button has been pressed.

Release Types

Natural release. Natural release occurs when you allow the pressure inside the pot to release gradually by letting the device cool down. When the float valve drops, often after 10 to 40 minutes, natural release is complete. Some of the recipes in this book call for a natural release for a certain number of minutes, and then the steam release handle is turned to the Venting position to release the remaining pressure quickly.

Quick release. When cooking time is complete, turn the steam release handle to the Venting position to quickly release all of the pressure inside the pot at one time. Once the float valve drops, you can safely open the lid.

Intermittent pressure release. This method is used for starchy foods. The idea is that you release a little pressure at a time to keep the valve from spitting out the starch and making a mess. Turn the steam release handle partway and hold it to release some pressure, then move the handle a little closer to the Venting position and hold to release more pressure.

MY FAVORITE ACCESSORIES

Springform pans

Mini round pan (6- or 7-inch) [15cm or 18cm]

7-inch (18cm) tube pan

Ramekins—6-ounce (175ml) are best

Wooden spoon

Silicone mini mitts

Steamer basket

Silicone trivet with long handles

Soup Socks™, a disposable mesh bag to hold vegetables and meat in broth

Glass lid, but you can also use one you already have, if it fits perfectly

Silicone egg bite mold to make mini "omelettes"

Rack for eggs

Care and Cleaning of Your Instant Pot®

The inner pot, lid, and steam rack are all dishwasher safe or can be hand-washed with normal dish soap.

Remove the silicone ring and wash it with soapy water. Dry it well before putting it back on the lid.

Clean the outside of the device with a sponge or cloth that was immersed in warm soapy water and has been thoroughly wrung out.

Altitude

If your machine does not adjust automatically for altitude, you need to increase cooking time. Some models of IP® allow you to program your altitude, and the appliance then adjusts the cooking time. Add 15 percent more cooking time at 5,000 feet (1500m) and then an additional 5 percent more time for every additional 1,000 feet (300m) of altitude.

USING YOUR INSTANT POT®
FOR KOSHER COOKING

Keeping kosher involves following dietary guidelines under Jewish law. There are foods that kosher people are not permitted to eat, such as shellfish and pork products. Permitted animals and poultry are kosher only if they are slaughtered and prepared according to strict laws, and there are certain parts of kosher animals that are also forbidden to eat.

One of the key aspects of kosher dietary laws (also known as the laws of kashrut) is the separation of dairy and meat. Poultry is considered meat, for example, while eggs and fish are considered neither poultry nor meat and are deemed "parve."

Always consult your own rabbinic authority on matters relating to your own kosher kitchen, but here are some basics.

For the kosher kitchen, following the laws of kashrut means that you must have two completely separate sets of dishes and utensils (one to be used with meat, the other with dairy), creating a very jammed kitchen, and many of us also have completely separate sets of dairy and meat dishes and utensils for Passover.

Many kosher kitchens also have parve utensils that are used for ingredients that are not dairy or meat, such as salad spinners, bowls, cutting boards, juicers, knives, and more. Foods prepared with parve utensils may be consumed on either dairy or meat plates.

When it comes to small appliances, we need separate ones as well. So that means separate blenders, mixers, and food processors. Many people keep their small appliances parve so they do not have to purchase and store so many of them.

The first question kosher people ask about the Instant Pot® is whether the appliance can be used for both dairy and meat. Since the food only touches the inner pot and the lid, one opinion is that you can use the same device for both dairy and meat but with two separate inner pots and lids. By the time you buy a second inner pot and lid, the cost is the same as buying an entirely separate IP®.

You should consult your own rabbinic authority on this matter, but all of the kosher people I know have separate devices for dairy and meat. I highly recommend having two. I love making breakfast and other dairy recipes in my Instant Pot®, and the recipe for New York Cheesecake (page 185) is one of the creamiest I have ever eaten.

Another issue is whether one can consume a parve dish prepared in a meat IP® with a dairy meal, and vice versa. The rabbinic experts I asked said yes, as long as the IP® had not been used for meat or dairy for 24 hours prior to being used for the parve dish.

It is the tradition in some communities to *toivel*, or immerse, new dishes in a dish *mikveh*, a ritual bath for dishes and utensils. To perform the *mitzvah* of *tevilas keilim*, the item is immersed in the water and a prayer is recited. The inner pot and the lid may be submerged in water to be *toiveled*.

The lid of the Instant Pot® is electric, and you cannot open it on Shabbat without trig- gering a beeping sound, so before you light candles, remove the lid and substitute a glass cover after your dish is fully cooked. Instant Pot® makes one that fits perfectly. The food can sit on the Warm setting for dinner, but if the meal is intended for Shabbat lunch, use the Slow Cook setting. As an alternative, the inner pot can be placed on a hot plate to keep warm.

Ingredient Tips

Oil. When recipes call for oil, you can use canola, sunflower, safflower, or grapeseed oil.

Eggs. All of the recipes in this book use LARGE eggs.

Salt. Unless stated otherwise, use fine sea salt.

Milk substitutes. You can use oat, soy, almond, cashew, or other nut milks as a substitute for milk.

SUGGESTED DISHES FOR HOLIDAYS

Rosh Hashanah

Moroccan Carrot Salad – 18

Gefilte Loaf – 34

Classic Chicken Soup
with Herbed Matzoh Balls – 47

Spinach Pesto Brisket – 115

Coq au Vin – 88

Kasha Varnishkes – 152

Tzimmis – 153

Potato Kugel – 154

Mom's Apple Raisin Noodle Kugel – 158

Honey Cake with Coffee
and Honey Glaze – 174

Thanksgiving

Butternut Squash Soup – 61

Turkey for Four – 97

Garlic Mashed Potatoes – 156

Cranberry and Orange Sauce – 169

Berry Compote – 187

Chanukah

Jewish Meets Irish Corned Beef
and Potatoes – 98

Applesauce – 179

Purim

Jeweled Israeli Couscous – 161

Persian Lamb and Herb Stew – 117

Passover

Lox, Egg, and Onion Bites – 3

Chimichurri Breakfast Potatoes – 4

Orange Shakshuka – 6

Broccoli, Cheddar, and Chive
Crustless Quiche – 8

Matzoh Brei Brûlée – 11

Beet and Mint Salad – 17

Moroccan Carrot Salad – 18

Turkish Eggplant Salad – 20

Passover Celery Root Salad – 22

Harissa-Spiced Quick Pickles – 25

Grandma's Creamy Potato Salad – 26

Gefilte Loaf – 34

Moroccan Fish Stew – 35

Swedish Meatballs – 38

Vegetable Stock – 44

Classic Chicken Soup
with Herbed Matzoh Balls – 47

Beef Bone Broth – 49

Indian Spiced Carrot Soup – 51

Golden Tomato Soup – 52

Shavuot

BREAKFAST
AND BRUNCH

Steel-Cut Oatmeal — 2

Lox, Egg, and Onion Bites — 3

Chimichurri Breakfast Potatoes — 4

Orange Shakshuka — 6

Broccoli, Cheddar, and Chive Crustless Quiche — 8

Matzoh Brei Brûlée — 11

Cheesy Grits — 13

STEEL-CUT OATMEAL

GLUTEN-FREE, PARVE

HANDS-ON TIME:	1 Minute
TIME TO PRESSURE:	9 Minutes
COOKING TIME:	5 Minutes
BUTTON TO USE:	Pressure Cook
RELEASE TYPE:	Natural Release for 10 to 15 Minutes
ADVANCE PREP:	May be made 5 days in advance

Serves 4, may be doubled

Oatmeal is one of those foods where the Instant Pot® really shines. I was always too lazy to cook steel-cut oats because it took too long, though I love the texture. I like my oatmeal thick, so I do the natural release for 15 minutes; if you prefer it wetter, let it sit for 10 minutes. The oatmeal will thicken up when stored in the fridge. I make this every Monday morning so I have it for breakfast the whole week. I eat it with a bit of brown sugar, fresh berries, and some of the foam from the frothed almond milk I prepare for my cappuccino.

1 cup (160g) steel-cut oats

3 cups (710ml) water

pinch salt, optional

FAVORITE ADDITIONS:

Milk, especially milk foamed in a frother

brown sugar

cinnamon

turmeric

fresh berries

dried fruit

Place the oats, water, and salt, if using, in the inner pot. Secure the lid, ensuring that the steam release handle is in the Sealing position. Press the Pressure Cook button and set the cooking time for 5 minutes.

When the cooking time is complete, let sit for 10 to 15 minutes to naturally release the pressure, depending on how wet or thick you like your oatmeal. Turn the steam release handle to the Venting position to release any remaining pressure. Press Cancel. Remove the lid. Mix in any of the additions you like.

LOX, EGG, AND ONION BITES

DAIRY OR PARVE,
GLUTEN-FREE, PASSOVER

HANDS ON TIME: 3 Minutes

TIME TO PRESSURE: 6 Minutes

COOKING TIME: 8 Minutes

BUTTON TO USE: Pressure Cook

RELEASE TYPE: Natural Release
for 8 Minutes

ADVANCE PREP: May be made
2 days in advance

Makes 7 bites

When I was growing up, my dad made only three things in the kitchen: roasted chestnuts, homemade grape jelly, and scrambled eggs and onions. He would have loved this super easy preparation of eggs. These are great snacks to have around.

5 large eggs

¼ cup (59ml) milk, or any milk substitute

1 green onion, sliced thinly

3 ounces (85g) smoked salmon, cut into ⅓- to ½-inch (8–13mm) pieces

⅛ teaspoon salt, or more to taste

⅛ teaspoon black pepper, or more to taste

1 cup (236ml) water

spray oil

Place the eggs and milk into a 2-cup (500ml) measuring cup or medium bowl and whisk well. Add the salt and pepper and mix well. Take a silicone egg bite mold and spray the insides of the molds with oil. Divide the green onions and salmon among the seven openings. Pour the egg batter into the molds, on top of the onions and salmon, about three-quarters full. Cover the entire mold pan with foil.

Pour the water into the inner pot. Place the steam rack on the counter and the egg bite mold on top. Lift the handles of the rack and press against the pan to secure it and lift up and place into the pot. Secure the lid, ensuring that the steam release handle is in the Sealing position. Press the Pressure Cook button and set the cooking time for 8 minutes.

When the cooking time is complete, let the pot sit for 8 minutes to naturally release the pressure. Turn the steam release handle to the Venting position to release any remaining pressure. Press Cancel. Remove the lid. Lift up the rack along with the mold. Remove the foil and turn the bites onto a plate to serve.

MEASURING CUPS

I am a huge fan of my 2-, 4-, and 8-cup (500ml, 1 liter, 2 liter) glass measuring cups and use them all the time to measure liquids. For this recipe, you want to be able to easily pour the batter into the molds, so the 2- or 4-cup (500ml or 1 liter) measuring cup with a spout works great.

CHIMICHURRI BREAKFAST POTATOES

This recipe is inspired by potatoes I ate at a trendy Los Angeles brunch spot. I loved that the potatoes were brightened up by a fresh green sauce. The IP® cooks the potatoes perfectly, and the best feature is that the potatoes are dry when you open the lid so they brown really well in the pan. Please do not be deterred by the extra step to brown the potatoes outside of the IP® after cooking them—trust me, you want them crispy. These are best made just before serving although they are also good as leftovers. They reheat well in a frying pan on medium-high heat.

Pour the water into the inner pot. Add the steam rack. Place the potatoes into a steamer basket and place on top of the rack or use a large steamer basket with feet. Secure the lid, ensuring that the steam release handle is in the Sealing position. Press the Pressure Cook button and set the cooking time for 5 minutes.

While the potatoes are cooking, make the sauce. In a food processor or blender, place the olive oil, vinegar, garlic, parsley, cilantro, oregano, red pepper flakes, and salt. Blend until you have a creamy sauce, scraping down the sides a few times. You get a creamier result if this is made in a blender.

When the cooking time is complete, turn the steam release handle to the Venting position to quickly release the pressure. Press Cancel and remove the lid.

GLUTEN-FREE, PARVE, PASSOVER, VEGAN

HANDS-ON TIME: 5 Minutes

TIME TO PRESSURE: 13 Minutes

COOKING TIME: 5 Minutes, plus 14 Minutes to brown the potatoes

BUTTONS TO USE: Pressure Cook

RELEASE TYPE: Quick Release

ADVANCE PREP: May be made 2 days in advance

Serves 6

1 cup (236ml) water

2 pounds (907g) Yukon Gold or Russet potatoes, cut into 1-inch (2.5cm) pieces

6 tablespoons (74ml) extra virgin olive oil

1 tablespoon red wine vinegar

4 cloves garlic

1 cup (25g) Italian parsley leaves

¼ cup (5g) cilantro leaves

2 teaspoons oregano

⅛ teaspoon red pepper flakes

½ teaspoon salt

3 tablespoons (30ml) oil, divided

kosher salt to taste

Heat 2 tablespoons of the oil in a large cast iron or non-stick pan over high heat. When hot, add half of the potatoes and let sit for 3 minutes, shaking the pan after 1 minute. Turn the potatoes over and cook for another 4 minutes, stirring a few times, until browned on all sides. Place into a serving bowl. Add another tablespoon of oil, wait 10 seconds, and add the remaining potatoes and cook as you did the first batch.

Place into the bowl. Mix in the chimichurri sauce. Add kosher salt to taste.

CHIMICHURRI SAUCE

You can also serve this sauce with the Whole Peruvian Spiced Chicken (page 80), brushed on the Garlic Corn on the Cob (page 164), or over asparagus (page 171), instead of the Lemon and Herb Sauce

ORANGE SHAKSHUKA

Shakshuka has been a staple of Israeli cuisine for decades, and now the rest of the world has discovered this dish, typically made by poaching eggs in a spicy tomato sauce. I cannot eat too much tomato sauce, so I created this recipe as my own twist on the classic. You can make between 4 and 6 eggs in this amount of sauce. Even when I am making 6 eggs, I do them in batches so the eggs are cooked right before serving. No one likes cold eggs.

Press Sauté and when the display reads "Hot," add the oil, onions, and peppers to the inner pot and cook for 3 to 4 minutes, stirring occasionally, until the onions are clear. Add the squash, sweet potato, turmeric, salt, and pepper and cook for 1 minute. Press Cancel.

Add the water and stir, scraping the bottom to ensure it is clean. Secure the lid, ensuring that the steam release handle is in the Sealing position. Press the Pressure Cook button and set the cooking time for 5 minutes.

Meanwhile, break three eggs into individual bowls. When the cooking time is complete, turn the steam release handle to the Venting position to quickly release the pressure. Press Cancel and remove the lid.

Use an immersion blender to partially purée the mixture, leaving some large pieces, but it should be mostly creamy. Stir the mixture.

GLUTEN-FREE, PARVE, PASSOVER

HANDS-ON TIME: 10 Minutes

TIME TO PRESSURE: 9 Minutes

COOKING TIME: 5 Minutes, plus 2 Minutes to cook the eggs

BUTTONS TO USE: Sauté and Pressure Cook

RELEASE TYPE: Quick Release

Serves 6

2 tablespoons extra virgin olive oil

1 small onion, cut into ¼-inch (6mm) pieces

1 yellow or orange pepper, cut into ½-inch (1.2cm) pieces

2 cups (about 700g) butternut squash cubes, cut into 1-inch (2.5cm) pieces

1 cup sweet potato cubes, cut into ½-inch (1.2cm) cubes, about two-thirds of a large sweet potato

¼ teaspoon turmeric

½ teaspoon salt

¼ teaspoon black pepper

⅓ cup (79ml) water

6 large eggs, divided

Press Sauté and press the button until the medium setting lights up. When the mixture starts to bubble, use a spoon to create three wells (holes) in the mixture. Slowly pour three of the eggs, one at a time, into the individual wells (one egg in each well). Cook for 2 minutes. Press Cancel. Secure the lid without locking the steam release handle and let sit for 4 to 5 minutes, until the eggs are set. Remove the lid and use a large spoon to scoop up an egg and the sauce to serve with it. Repeat with the remaining three eggs.

BROCCOLI, CHEDDAR, AND CHIVE CRUSTLESS QUICHE

DAIRY OR PARVE,
GLUTEN-FREE, PASSOVER

HANDS-ON TIME:	8 Minutes, quiche needs to sit for 10 Minutes
TIME TO PRESSURE:	10 Minutes
COOKING TIME:	30 Minutes
BUTTON TO USE:	Pressure Cook
RELEASE TYPE:	Natural Release for 8 Minutes
ADVANCE PREP:	May be made 2 days in advance

Serves 6–8

This was a big hit for brunch for a small group. For the broccoli, start chopping the florets first and measure out the 1½ cups (354ml), and add chopped stems if needed.

Take a 7-inch (18cm) soufflé dish or a 6 × 3-inch (15 × 7.5cm) round cake pan and trace a circle on parchment paper. Cut out the circle about ¼ inch (6mm) inside the line. Spray the bottom and sides of the dish with oil, insert the parchment circle, and then spray the top of the parchment paper. Set aside.

In a large bowl place the eggs and milk and whisk well. Add the shallots, chives, lemon zest, salt, and pepper and whisk well. Add the broccoli and cheese and mix well. Pour into the prepared dish. Pour the water into the inner pot and add the steam rack.

Create an aluminum foil sling (see page xi). Place the pan on top of the sling and place the dish on top. Use the sides of the sling to lift the pan and place it into the inner pot on top of the rack. Fold the top of the sling over the top of the pan.

Secure the lid, ensuring that the steam release handle is in the Sealing position. Press the Pressure Cook button and set the cooking time for 30 minutes.

spray oil

6 large eggs

½ cup (118ml) milk, or milk substitute

1 small shallot, chopped into ¼-inch (6mm) pieces, about 3 heaping tablespoons chopped

20 chives, cut with a scissors into ¼-inch (6mm) pieces

1 teaspoon lemon zest

½ teaspoon salt

⅛ teaspoon black pepper

2 cups (473ml) chopped broccoli, chopped into ¾-inch (20mm) pieces maximum, about 6 ounces (170g) of broccoli crowns

1 cup (112g) shredded cheddar cheese

1 cup (236ml) water

When the cooking time is complete, let the pot sit for 8 minutes to naturally release the pressure. Turn the steam release handle to the Venting position to release any remaining pressure.

Lift the sides of the sling to remove the quiche and let sit for 10 minutes. Run a thin knife around the edges of the quiche. Place a plate on top of the pan to turn the quiche out of the dish and then turn the quiche over onto a serving plate.

FAVORITE TOOLS: KITCHEN SCISSORS

I love my kitchen scissors and have one pair for meat and one for dairy as I use them so often. They are useful for cutting herbs such as chives and for cutting chicken into pieces as well as to cut out parchment paper circles to line pans.

MATZOH BREI BRÛLÉE

DAIRY, PASSOVER

HANDS-ON TIME: 8 Minutes

TIME TO PRESSURE: 6 Minutes

COOKING TIME: 27 Minutes, plus 3 Minutes to brûlée the top

BUTTON TO USE: Pressure Cook

RELEASE TYPE: Natural Release for 10 Minutes

Serves 4–6

I know what you're thinking, but really the only three reasons to make matzoh brei in the Instant Pot® are (1) you can, (2) there is no need to stand over the pan, and (3) you'll have reduced cleanup this way. I also really liked the texture of it.

4 squares of matzoh

1 cup (236ml) half and half

1 tablespoon (14g) butter, for greasing pan

6 large eggs

2 tablespoons brown sugar

2 teaspoons ground cinnamon

2 teaspoons pure vanilla extract

¼ teaspoon salt

1 cup (236ml) water

2 tablespoons sugar, to brûlée the top

Break the matzoh into 2-inch (5cm) pieces and place into a large bowl. Pour the half and half over them and turn to coat. Let sit for 5 minutes, moving the bottom matzoh pieces to the top and pressing the matzoh a few times to moisten all the pieces.

Place a large piece of foil on top of the bottom piece of a 7-inch (18cm) springform pan and fold the excess foil under the pan bottom. Attach the outer side section of the pan, lock it in place, and then take the part of the foil that you folded under the pan and wrap it up and around the outside of the pan. Grease the bottom and sides of the pan with the butter. Set aside.

Meanwhile, in another bowl, place the eggs, brown sugar, cinnamon, vanilla, and salt and whisk well.

Use your hands to lift the matzoh out of the half and half and place it into the pan. Add the egg mixture to the remaining half and half in the bowl that held the matzoh and whisk well. Pour over the matzoh. Cover with aluminum foil.

Place the water into the inner pot and add the steam rack. Create an aluminum foil sling (see page xi). Place the pan on top of the sling and use the sides to lift the dish and place on top of the steam rack in the pot. Fold the top of the sling over the top of the pan. Press the Pressure Cook button and set the cooking time for 27 minutes.

When the cooking time is complete, let the pot sit for 10 minutes to naturally release the pressure. Turn the valve to the Venting position to release any remaining pressure.

Remove the foil on top of the pan. Place the pan on top of a cookie sheet and set the oven to broil. Sprinkle the sugar on top of the matzoh brei and then broil for about 3 minutes, watching carefully so the sugar doesn't burn. Unlock the pan and remove the sides. Use a spatula to separate the matzoh brei from the pan bottom and move to a serving plate.

MATZOH BREI

Matzoh brei will always remind me of my mother, because she made it every Passover. She always ate it, just like she did her pancakes, slathered in raspberry jam rather than syrup. If you are making it for a buffet, serve it with several types of jam in bowls along with maple syrup.

CHEESY GRITS

DAIRY, GLUTEN-FREE

HANDS-ON TIME: 4 Minutes

TIME TO PRESSURE: 8 Minutes

COOKING TIME: 10 Minutes

BUTTONS TO USE: Sauté and Pressure Cook

RELEASE TYPE: Natural Release for 15 Minutes

ADVANCE PREP: May be made 3 days in advance

Serves 4–6

Yes, I know than I'm a Yankee through and through, but I also live in Maryland, so I am *almost* in the south. I tasted my first cheesy grits in Chicago, at a fancy hotel, at the urging of my late friend Suzin Glickman, *z"l*, who, like me, was also born in Long Island. One taste and I was hooked. So don't knock them until you try them. You can use any cheese you like, but the stronger the flavor, the better.

2 tablespoons (28g) butter

1 cup (112g) corn grits, not the quick-cooking kind

½ teaspoon salt, or more to taste

3 cups (710ml) water

1 cup (236ml) half and half, plus another ¼ cup (59ml) or more for serving, if you like it creamier

1 cup (108g) shredded Gruyere or other sharp cheese

Press Sauté and when the display reads "Hot," add the butter to the inner pot. Once melted, add the grits and cook for 2 minutes, stirring almost the entire time. Press Cancel. Add the salt, water, and 1 cup (236ml) of the half and half and stir, making sure the bottom is clean. Secure the lid, ensuring that the steam release handle is in the Sealing position. Press the Pressure Cook button and set the cooking time for 10 minutes.

When the cooking time is complete, let the pot sit for 15 minutes to naturally release the pressure. Turn the steam release handle to the Venting position to release any remaining pressure. Use a wooden spoon to stir the mixture until creamy. Sprinkle in the cheese a little at a time and mix in well. Add more cream if you like it creamier and more salt to taste. The grits thicken as they cool.

When serving, you can make them even cheesier if you grate some more cheese right on top in your bowl. To reheat the next day, add a bit of cream or milk to the thickened grits before reheating.

SALADS, DIPS, AND APPETIZERS

BEET AND MINT SALAD

This simple beet salad is perfect served with gefilte fish, Shabbat lunch, or whenever you just want to take a prepared dish out of the fridge to serve at room temperature. You can make this a few days in advance, but add the remaining mint leaves before serving.

GLUTEN-FREE, PARVE,
PASSOVER, VEGAN

HANDS-ON TIME: 4 Minutes, plus
10 Minutes to cool
beets

TIME TO PRESSURE: 9 Minutes

COOKING TIME: 30 Minutes

BUTTON TO USE: Pressure Cook

RELEASE TYPE: Quick Release

ADVANCE PREP: May be made 3 days
in advance

Serves 8

Place the water into the inner pot and insert the steam rack. Place the beets on top. Secure the lid, ensuring that the steam release handle is in the Sealing position. Press the Pressure Cook button and set the cooking time for 30 minutes. When the cooking time is complete, turn the steam release handle to the Venting position to quickly release the pressure. Press Cancel and remove the lid.

Remove the beets to a colander and let them cool for 10 minutes. Use gloved hands to rub the skins off of the beets. Cut the beets into 1-inch (2.5cm) cubes and place into a large serving bowl.

Meanwhile, place the oil, orange juice, red onions, half of the mint leaves, 1 tablespoon water, and the salt and pepper into a small bowl and whisk well. Add the orange pieces and stir. Add to the beets and mix well. When ready to serve, add the remaining mint leaves.

1 cup (236ml) water

4 medium beets, about 2 pounds (907g), scrubbed clean

2 tablespoons extra virgin olive oil

1 large navel orange, sliced in half; remove the flesh from half and cut it into ½-inch (1.2cm) pieces, and then juice the other half

2 tablespoons chopped red onion, about one-quarter of 1 small red onion

12 large mint leaves, chopped

1 tablespoon water

¼ teaspoon salt

¼ teaspoon black pepper

MOROCCAN CARROT SALAD

In December 2018, our family went to Morocco for vacation and took a cooking class outside Marrakesh. For years I had chopped my carrots for this salad into circles, but our teacher, Chef Tariq, said that the classic method is to cut the carrots into cubes.

Place the steam rack inside the inner pot and add the water. Pile the carrots on top of the rack, the thickest ones at the bottom. Secure the lid, ensuring that the steam release handle is in the Sealing position. Press the Pressure Cook button and set the cooking time for 2 minutes.

While the carrots are cooking, place the oil and garlic into a small bowl and stir. In a large bowl, place the lemon juice, cumin, salt, and pepper and stir. When the cooking time is complete, turn the steam release handle to the Venting position to quickly release the pressure. Press Cancel and remove the lid.

Place the carrots into a colander and rinse with cold water. Place on a clean dishtowel to dry. Once the carrots are cool enough to handle, slice each in half the long way, and then into quarters the long way (for skinny carrots, just halve). Slice into ½- to ¾-inch (1.2cm to 2cm) cubes and place into the large bowl. If your carrots are very thick, slice lengthwise into thirds. Stir.

GLUTEN-FREE, PARVE, PASSOVER, VEGAN

HANDS-ON TIME: 6 Minutes, tastes best if chilled for 1 hour

TIME TO PRESSURE: 12 Minutes

COOKING TIME: 2 Minutes

BUTTON TO USE: Pressure Cook

RELEASE TYPE: Quick Release

ADVANCE PREP: May be made 2 days in advance

Serves 8–10

1 cup (236ml) water

2 pounds (907g) carrots, peeled and trimmed, very long ones cut in half to fit inside the pot

¼ cup (59ml) extra virgin olive oil

2 large cloves garlic, crushed

¼ cup (59ml) fresh lemon juice, from 1 to 2 lemons

1½ teaspoons cumin

½ teaspoon kosher salt, or more to taste

½ teaspoon black pepper, or more to taste

¾ cup (18g) cilantro leaves, dried well, chopped roughly

Strain the oil over the carrots, discarding the garlic, and mix well. Taste and add more salt and pepper if needed. Add the cilantro and mix again. Place into the fridge for at least 1 hour for the flavors to come together. Mix again and serve.

MOROCCAN CARROT SALAD

For a spicier version, add red pepper flakes to taste.

TURKISH EGGPLANT SALAD

GLUTEN-FREE, PARVE,
PASSOVER, VEGAN

HANDS-ON TIME:	18 Minutes, best served after it has been chilled for 2 hours.
TIME TO PRESSURE:	4 Minutes
COOKING TIME:	6 Minutes
RELEASE TYPE:	Quick Release
BUTTONS TO USE:	Sauté and Pressure Cook
ADVANCE PREP:	May be made 2 days in advance

I am a huge fan of cooked eggplant salads as you can make them in advance and the taste gets better every day. You could serve this as a warm side dish as well, but I prefer it chilled and served as a salad.

Press Sauté and when the display reads "Hot," add 2 tablespoons of the oil to the inner pot. Add half of the eggplant and cook for 4 to 5 minutes, turning a few times to brown; the eggplant does not have to be fully cooked, just browned. Remove to a plate. Add 2 more tablespoons of the oil, wait a few seconds, and then add the remaining eggplant pieces and brown for 4 more minutes, turning to brown all sides. Remove to the plate.

Add the remaining oil to the pan and add the onions, celery, garlic, and pine nuts. Cook for 4 minutes, stirring occasionally, until the onions are translucent. Add the raisins, cumin, red pepper flakes, salt, and pepper and stir. Add the water and use a wooden spoon to scrape up anything stuck to the bottom of the pot.

Press Cancel. Return the eggplant to the pan and mix well. Place the tomatoes on top, without stirring. Let cool and place in the fridge for 2 hours or overnight.

Serves 6–8

6 tablespoons (90ml) extra virgin olive oil, divided

1 large eggplant, cut into 1½-inch (4cm) cubes

1 large onion, chopped into ½-inch (1.2cm) cubes

2 stalks celery, cut into ½-inch (1.2cm) cubes

4 cloves garlic, roughly chopped

¼ cup (34g) pine nuts

¼ cup (41g) golden raisins

1 teaspoon cumin

¼ teaspoon red pepper flakes

1 teaspoon salt

¼ teaspoon black pepper

1 tablespoon water

ingredients continue on following page

Secure the lid, ensuring that the steam release handle is in the Sealing position. Press the Pressure Cook button and set the cooking time for 6 minutes. When the cooking time is complete, turn the steam release handle to the Venting position to quickly release the pressure. Press Cancel and remove the lid.

Press Sauté and cook for 3 minutes, stirring occasionally, to reduce the liquid. Add more salt and black pepper as needed. Let cool and then refrigerate until cold, a few hours or overnight. Before serving, sprinkle the parsley on top.

2 medium tomatoes, quartered, seeded, and chopped into 1-inch (2.5cm) pieces

1 tablespoon chopped parsley, for garnish

SEEDING TOMATOES

Cut the tomato into quarters and then use your fingers to scoop out and discard the seeds.

PASSOVER CELERY ROOT SALAD

GLUTEN-FREE, PARVE,
PASSOVER, VEGAN

HANDS-ON TIME:	9 Minutes, salad needs to chill for 3 hours
COOKING TIME:	0 Minutes
BUTTONS TO USE:	Sauté and Pressure Cook
RELEASE TYPE:	Quick Release
ADVANCE PREP:	May be made 2 days in advance

Serves 6–8

Susan Barocas is a friend and fellow food writer in the Washington, DC, area, known for her cooking classes full of Sephardic culinary history. She prepares a version of this salad every Passover to honor her Turkish ancestry. When I told her that I wanted to create a version for the Instant Pot®, which she had never used, we came up with the recipe below. Susan loved the idea of taking a traditional recipe and adapting it for a modern device. You can serve this any time.

½ cup (118ml) fresh lemon juice, from 2 lemons

5 cups (1.2 liters) water, divided

2 large celery roots

⅓ cup (79ml) extra virgin olive oil

⅓ cup (5g) fresh dill

1 tablespoon sugar

½ teaspoon salt

¼ teaspoon black pepper

2 stalks celery, thinly sliced

¼ cup (5g) Italian parsley leaves, roughly chopped

Place half of the lemon juice and 4 cups (1 liter) of the water into a large bowl. Use a paring knife to remove and discard the outer layer of the celery root, leaving only the white part. Cut it into 1½-inch (4cm) pieces. Add to the bowl and submerge to prevent browning. When all of the celery root has been cut, lift the pieces out of the lemon water and place into the inner pot. Add the remaining lemon juice, the remaining 1 cup (236ml) of water, olive oil, dill, sugar, salt, and pepper and stir.

Secure the lid, ensuring that the steam release handle is in the Sealing position. Press the Pressure Cook button and set the cooking time for 0 minutes. When the cooking time is complete, press Cancel and turn the steam release handle to the Venting position to quickly release the pressure. Remove the lid.

Use a slotted spoon to remove the celery root pieces to a serving bowl. Pick out the dill and discard. Add the sliced celery and stir. Press Sauté, bring to a boil, and then cook the remaining liquid for 5 to 7 minutes, stirring often, until you have a thick sauce. Pour the sauce over the celery root pieces and stir. Add the parsley and stir. Cover and refrigerate for at least 3 hours before serving.

HARISSA-SPICED QUICK PICKLES

GLUTEN-FREE, PARVE, PASSOVER, VEGAN

HANDS-ON TIME: 3 Minutes

TIME TO PRESSURE: 7 Minutes

COOKING TIME: 1 Minute

BUTTON TO USE: Pressure Cook

RELEASE TYPE: Quick Release

ADVANCE PREP: May be made 1 week in advance

Harissa, a paste made of red chile peppers, is common in North African cooking. These pickles were a fun experiment one day, and my whole family was excited when we tasted them. You can also add more harissa if you want really spicy pickles.

Makes one jar of pickles.

⅔ cup (158ml) apple cider vinegar

1 cup (236ml) water

2 tablespoons sugar

1 tablespoon kosher salt

2 tablespoons pickling spices

1 cup (10g) fresh dill, divided

1 clove garlic, lightly smashed

½ teaspoon harissa; for pickles with a little kick, add more to taste

2 pickling cucumbers cut into coins with a wavy slicer

Place the vinegar, water, sugar, salt, pickling spices, half of the dill, garlic, and harissa into the inner pot. Secure the lid, ensuring that the steam release handle is in the Sealing position. Press the Pressure Cook button and set the cooking time for 1 minute. When the cooking time is complete, press Cancel. Turn the steam release handle to the Venting position to quickly release the pressure. Remove the lid.

Carefully lift the inner pot out of the device and let the pickling liquid cool for 3 minutes. Place the cucumbers into a large jar, such as an empty 24-ounce (680g) pasta sauce jar. Pour the cooking liquid over the cucumbers. Tuck in the remaining fresh dill. Store in the fridge at least overnight; they will taste better after a few days.

HUMMUS

Hummus made with cooked dry chickpeas is far superior to hummus made with canned chickpeas. The Instant Pot® makes this so quick and with no need to soak the chickpeas overnight.

GLUTEN-FREE, PARVE, VEGAN

HANDS-ON TIME: 5 Minutes

TIME TO PRESSURE: 12 Minutes

COOKING TIME: 50 Minutes

BUTTON TO USE: Pressure Cook

RELEASE TYPE: Quick Release

ADVANCE PREP: May be made 3 days in advance

Serves 6–8

Place the chickpeas, baking soda, and water into the inner pot. Stir. Secure the lid, ensuring that the steam release handle is in the Sealing position. Press the Pressure Cook button and set the cooking time for 50 minutes.

When you have about 15 minutes left on the chickpea cooking time, place the lemon juice into the food processor bowl and add the garlic, tahini, cumin, salt, and olive oil. Let sit until you are ready to add the cooked chickpeas.

When the cooking time is complete, turn the steam release handle to the Venting position to quickly release the pressure. Press Cancel and remove the lid. Drain the chickpeas, reserving the cooking liquid.

Add the chickpeas and ½ cup (118ml) of the cooking liquid to the processor bowl. Process until creamy, and add additional tablespoons of cooking liquid if the mixture is too thick and mix in.

Garnish with olive oil and sprinkle with sumac.

1 cup (170g) dry chickpeas

½ teaspoon baking soda

4 cups (1 liter) water

4 tablespoons lemon juice

4 cloves garlic

¼ cup (60g) tahini

1 teaspoon cumin

1 teaspoon salt

3 tablespoons extra virgin olive oil, plus more for garnish

½ cup (118ml) or more cooking liquid

sumac to taste

JUICING CITRUS

If you are a serious home cook, invest in either a heavy-gauge hand juicer or an electric one. I use the hand one if I am juicing one piece of citrus, but if I need more, I take out the electric one. To get more juice out of citrus, roll them on the counter to loosen the pulp or heat the citrus in the microwave oven for 30 to 45 seconds.

BEET TAHINI

This is a showstopper dish, as the red color looks unreal and is great for a buffet. I make this as a dip to serve with crudité, to shmear on challah or my homemade sourdough toast, or to dollop on my plate with smoked turkey. It's perfect for a BBQ as well. For another version, use yellow or orange beets and add turmeric to the recipe for a gorgeous yellow dip.

Place the water into the inner pot. Add the beets. Secure the lid, ensuring that the steam release handle is in the Sealing position. Press the Pressure Cook button and set the cooking time for 10 minutes. When the cooking time is complete, press Cancel. Turn the steam release handle to the Venting position to quickly release the pressure. Strain the beets over a bowl, reserving the cooking liquid.

Place the garlic into the bowl of a food processor and chop into small pieces. Scrape down the sides. Add the beets along with the lemon juice, tahini, cumin, salt, ⅓ cup (79ml) of the cooking liquid, and olive oil. If you are making yellow beet tahini, add the turmeric.

Process until creamy, scraping down the sides of the bowl a few times. If the mixture is too thick for your taste, add more cooking liquid, 2 tablespoons at a time, and mix until smooth. Chill for at least 1 hour before serving with the garnish of your choice. I chill the cooking liquid and drink the beet juice the next day.

GLUTEN-FREE, PARVE, VEGAN

HANDS-ON TIME:	5 Minutes, plus 1 hour to chill before serving
TIME TO PRESSURE:	9 Minutes
COOKING TIME:	10 Minutes
BUTTON TO USE:	Pressure Cook
RELEASE TYPE:	Quick Release
ADVANCE PREP:	May be made 3 days in advance.

Makes 2½ cups

1½ (354ml) cups water

2 medium beets, about 1 pound (454g), peeled and cut into 1-inch (2.5cm) cubes

2 cloves garlic

2 tablespoons fresh lemon juice, from 1 to 2 large lemons

½ cup (120g) tahini

1 teaspoon cumin

½ teaspoon salt

¼ cup (59ml) extra virgin olive oil

For yellow or orange beet tahini, add ½ teaspoon turmeric, or more for a stronger yellow color

OPTIONAL GARNISH:

drizzle of olive oil

toasted pine nuts

Italian parsley leaves

DOLMAS WITH BEEF AND MINT

GLUTEN-FREE, MEAT

HANDS-ON TIME:	25 Minutes
TIME TO PRESSURE:	10 Minutes
COOKING TIME:	20 Minutes
BUTTON TO USE:	Pressure Cook
RELEASE TYPE:	Natural Release for 5 minutes
ADVANCE PREP:	May be made 3 days in advance or frozen

Makes 43 rolls

I spend a lot of time in my kitchen by myself developing recipes, with music, a podcast, or an old bingeable TV series in the background to keep me company. When I tested this recipe, my friend Paula Jacobson, recipe editor and tester extraordinaire, came by for lunch, and together we rolled up all 43 of these cuties one by one. Neither of us had ever made stuffed grape leaves before, and we just figured it out together. They turned out really tasty and are a great snack to have in the fridge, as well as part of a nice Shabbat or holiday appetizer of mezze, along with Beet Tahini (page 31) and Turkish Eggplant Salad (page 20).

½ cup (90g) basmati rice

1 cup (236ml) hot water

1 jar grape leaves

1 pound (454g) ground beef

1 medium onion, chopped fine or minced in a food processor

3 tablespoons chopped fresh dill

3 tablespoons chopped fresh mint leaves

2 cloves garlic, crushed

1 tablespoon oil

1 teaspoon allspice

¼ teaspoon salt

¼ teaspoon black pepper

1 cup (236ml) water

½ cup (118ml) fresh lemon juice, from 3 lemons

Place the rice into a medium bowl and add the hot water. Let sit for 10 minutes. Meanwhile, remove the grape leaves from the jar and place into a large colander. Separate them, rinse well, and place on a clean dishtowel. Drain the rice.

Place the rice, beef, onions, dill, mint, garlic, oil, allspice, salt, and pepper into a large bowl and use your hands to knead the ingredients together.

Separate the larger grape leaves to fill and set aside the smaller ones. Place a large grape leaf on a paper towel in front of you and fan out the leaf. Scoop up a level tablespoon of the filling and shape into a horizontal 2-inch (5cm) log at the bottom of the center vein. Lift up the two parts of the leaf that are below the filling and fold up over the filling; the center of the filling log will be exposed. Fold the right and left sides of the leaf toward the middle over the filling, and then roll up, tucking in any parts of the leaf to get a pretty roll. You do not need to fold too tightly. Place onto a plate and repeat until you have used up the filling.

Place the water into the pot. Cover the bottom of the pot with about 20 of the small, unfilled grape leaves, overlapping, to make a bed for the filled rolls to sit on. Place the rolls on top of the leaves next to each other in rows in one direction, and then place a second layer on top but in the other direction. Pour the lemon juice on top.

Secure the lid, ensuring that the steam release handle is in the Sealing position. Press the Pressure Cook button and set the cooking time for 20 minutes. When the cooking time is complete, let the pot sit to naturally release the pressure for 5 minutes. Turn the steam release handle to the Venting position to release any remaining pressure.

Enjoy hot or cold.

MIXING GROUND BEEF

Whenever you are making hamburgers, meatloaf, meatballs, or any ground beef or chicken mixture, the best way to mix and distribute the ingredients is to knead them with your hands for several minutes.

GEFILTE LOAF

PARVE, PASSOVER

HANDS-ON TIME: 6 Minutes, needs to chill overnight

TIME TO PRESSURE: 12 Minutes

COOKING TIME: 20 Minutes

BUTTON TO USE: Pressure Cook

RELEASE TYPE: Quick Release

ADVANCE PREP: May be made 2 days in advance

Serves 8–10

Years ago I made gefilte fish from scratch and served it to my father at the Seder. He said that he liked it. The next night we went to my neighbor Judith Gold's for dinner, and she served a frozen, sliced loaf. My father went on and on about how much he liked Judith's gefilte better than mine—he didn't realize that it wasn't homemade.

Place the carrots, onions, and peppercorns into the inner pot. Add the water and lemon slices. Press Sauté and when the liquid comes to a boil, press Cancel. Remove the plastic wrapping from the loaf but leave on the parchment paper wrapping. Place the loaf into the liquid.

Secure the lid, ensuring that the steam release handle is in the Sealing position. Press the Pressure Cook button and set the cooking time for 20 minutes. When the cooking time is complete, turn the steam release handle to the Venting position to quickly release the pressure. Remove the lid. Lift the loaf onto a serving dish or pan and add the carrots. Let cool and then refrigerate overnight. To serve, slice the loaf and place onto a platter or plate. Place a carrot on top of each.

2 carrots, peeled and sliced into coins

1 onion, quartered

1 teaspoon black peppercorns

3 cups (710ml) water

1 lemon, sliced

1 (22-ounce [624g]) frozen gefilte fish loaf

MOROCCAN FISH STEW

GLUTEN-FREE, PARVE, PASSOVER

HANDS-ON TIME:	10 Minutes, chill for at least 5 hours before serving
TIME TO PRESSURE:	11 Minutes
COOKING TIME:	3 Minutes
BUTTONS TO USE:	Sauté and Pressure Cook
RELEASE TYPE:	Quick Release
ADVANCE PREP:	May be made 1 day in advance

This is basically the Sephardic version of gefilte fish—the first course fish preparation served in all Moroccan and other Sephardi homes on Friday nights. For more kick, you can add more red pepper flakes. I recall having a delicious version of this recipe in Panama at a Shabbat dinner with friends.

Serves 6–8 as an appetizer

Press Sauté and when the display reads "Hot," add the oil, red peppers, onions, and garlic to the inner pot and cook for 4 minutes, stirring often. Add the water and use a wooden spoon to scrape the bottom of the pot clean. Add the lemon juice, paprika, coriander, cumin, crushed tomatoes, harissa, and red pepper flakes and stir. Bring to a boil. Stir the bottom again to make sure nothing is sticking.

Scoop up 1 cup (236ml) of the sauce. Add the fish to the pot and pour the reserved sauce on top. Secure the lid, ensuring that the steam release handle is in the Sealing position. Press the Pressure Cook button and set the cooking time for 3 minutes. When the cooking time is complete, turn the steam release handle to the Venting position to quickly release the pressure. Press Cancel and remove the lid.

Transfer the fish to a 9 × 13-inch (23 × 33cm) serving dish, moving the fish carefully so that the filets do not fall apart. Spoon sauce all over the fish so that all the pieces are submerged. Let cool and then refrigerate for 5 hours or overnight. Remove from the refrigerator about 20 minutes before serving so that it is room temperature when eaten.

2 tablespoons extra virgin olive oil

1 red pepper, sliced thinly

1 medium onion, halved and sliced

6 cloves garlic, chopped roughly

1/2 cup (118ml) water

1/4 cup (59ml) fresh lemon juice, from about 1–2 lemons

1 tablespoon paprika

1 teaspoon coriander

1/2 teaspoon cumin

1 cup (236ml) crushed tomatoes

1/3 cup (84g or 79ml) harissa

1/2 teaspoon crushed red pepper flakes, or more for a spicier dish

1 teaspoon salt

1 1/2 pounds (680g) white fish halved the long way, about 7 tilapia filets

CHICKEN SALAD WITH JAPANESE GINGER DRESSING

GLUTEN-FREE, MEAT

HANDS-ON TIME: 7 Minutes

TIME TO PRESSURE: 6 Minutes

COOKING TIME: 15 Minutes

BUTTON TO USE: Pressure Cook

RELEASE TYPE: Quick Release

ADVANCE PREP: Chicken may be made 2 days in advance, and dressing may be made 4 days in advance

STORE: Store chicken in the fridge for up to 3 days and dressing for up to 5 days

This is a super easy recipe to make for a healthy lunch or appetizer. It is amazing to cook with frozen chicken because you do not have to plan in advance. You can make this with fresh chicken as well, and the device will come to pressure more quickly. This is a dressing you can use on any salad.

Makes 1½ cups (354ml) dressing
Serves 4 people as a main course
and 6–8 as a first course

To make the chicken, place the water, garlic, mustard seeds, and peppercorns into the inner pot. Insert the steam rack and place the frozen chicken breasts on top. Secure the lid, ensuring that the steam release handle is in the Sealing position. Press the Pressure Cook button and set the cooking time for 15 minutes.

Meanwhile, to make the dressing, place the carrots, onion, oil, ginger, sugar, soy sauce, vinegar, and salt into a blender or food processor. Process until completely puréed.

When the cooking time is complete, turn the steam release handle to the Venting position to quickly release the pressure. Press Cancel and remove the lid.

Place the chicken on a plate and use two forks to shred.

CHICKEN

1 cup (236ml) water

2 cloves garlic, peeled

½ teaspoon mustard seeds

½ teaspoon black peppercorns

3 boneless chicken breasts, about 1.3 pounds (590g) total, breasts separated by rinsing in cold water and then pulled apart

ingredients continue on following page

To prepare the salad, place the greens, radishes, green onions, fennel, tomatoes, and avocado into a large bowl. Add the shredded chicken and dressing, a little at a time, until everything is coated. You may not need to use all the dressing.

DRESSING

2 medium carrots, peeled and cut into thirds

½ medium onion, halved

½ cup (118ml) oil

1 tablespoon chopped fresh ginger, about a 1-inch (2.5cm) piece

4 teaspoons sugar

2 tablespoons soy sauce

¼ cup (59ml) rice vinegar

¼ teaspoon salt

SALAD

8 cups (about 5 ounces [142g]) packed spinach, arugula or mesclun blend

2 radishes, sliced thinly

3 green onions, sliced

1 fennel bulb, sliced thinly

½ cup (about 75g) grape tomatoes, halved

1 avocado, cubed

SWEDISH MEATBALLS

Testing this recipe made me smile and cry at the same time. This is a family favorite from my mother's side of the family. Both my mom and grandma rolled the meat mixture into tiny balls, maybe 1/2 teaspoon in diameter, but I do not have the patience for that so mine are 1 teaspoon wide. What made them extra special was that my dad actually made homemade grape jelly from grapes we grew in our garden in Long Beach, New York. As of the writing of this book, I still have one jar with his handwritten label in the cupboard. As he is gone, I cannot bring myself to use it. The meatballs are still delicious with store-bought jam, and the smell made me miss all of the family members who have a part in the story of these delicious meatballs. My mother always served them as an appetizer, but I often serve them as an extra-special main dish.

Place the onion and egg into a food processor and process until creamy. Place into a bowl. Add the meat, garlic, matzoh meal, salt, and pepper and mix well. I like to use gloved hands.

Scoop up a heaping teaspoon of the meat mixture at a time and roll into balls. Wet your hands if the meat is sticking to them. Place onto a plate.

Press Sauté and when the display reads "Hot," add the jar of chili sauce, jelly, and water, stir, and heat until boiling and the sauce is a uniform color. Press Cancel. Add the meatballs.

MEAT, PASSOVER

HANDS-ON TIME:	30 Minutes
TIME TO PRESSURE:	13 Minutes
COOKING TIME:	8 Minutes, plus 5 Minutes to cook down sauce
BUTTONS TO USE:	Sauté and Pressure Cook
RELEASE TYPE:	Natural Release for 10 Minutes
ADVANCE PREP:	May be made 3 days in advance or frozen

Serves 6–8 as first course

1 small onion, quartered

1 large egg

1 pound (454g) ground beef

2 cloves garlic, crushed

¼ cup (32g) matzoh meal

¼ teaspoon salt

¼ teaspoon black pepper

12 ounces (355ml) chili sauce (the tangy rather than the spicy kind)

1¼ cups (283g) grape jelly or jam

½ cup (118ml) water

Secure the lid, ensuring that the steam release handle is in the Sealing position. Press the Pressure Cook button and set the cooking time for 8 minutes. When the cooking time is complete, let the pot sit to naturally release the pressure for 10 minutes. Turn the steam release handle to the Venting position to release any remaining pressure. Press Cancel and open the lid.

Press Sauté and cook for 5 minutes to thicken the sauce, stirring occasionally.

EVERYTHING BAGEL
BBQ CHICKEN WINGS

GLUTEN-FREE, MEAT

HANDS-ON TIME: 1 Minute

TIME TO PRESSURE: 15–17 Minutes

COOKING TIME: 5 Minutes, plus broil for 10 Minutes

BUTTON TO USE: Pressure Cook

RELEASE TYPE: Quick Release

ADVANCE PREP: May be made 2 days in advance

Serves 6

Years ago I tested recipes for two of Susie Fishbein's cookbooks and learned that the best way to make chicken wings was to boil them first and then bake them. The IP® makes the process faster.

1 cup (236ml) water

3–4 pounds (1.3–1.8kg) chicken wings

1 cup (236ml) barbeque sauce

½ teaspoon black pepper

3–3½ tablespoons Everything Bagel spice, divided

Place the water into the inner pot and add the steam rack. Pile the wings on top.

Secure the lid, ensuring that the steam release handle is in the Sealing position. Press the Pressure Cook button and set the cooking time for 5 minutes. When the cooking time is complete, turn the steam release handle to the Venting position to quickly release the pressure. Preheat the oven to broil. Press Cancel and open the lid.

Remove the wings to a baking pan. Pour the barbeque sauce and pepper on top and toss to coat. Sprinkle half of the Everything Bagel spice on top. Place the pan into the oven on a rack in the top third of the oven, but not on the oven rack closest to the heat. Broil for 5 minutes. Turn the wings over, and add the remaining Everything Bagel spice and broil for another 5 minutes, or longer until desired browning.

SOUPS

VEGETABLE STOCK

If you want your food to be as natural as possible, then homemade stock is a must. The IP® makes it easy to make flavorful stock to freeze to have available for all the great soups, stews, and rice dishes in this book. If the vegetables do not fit in the pot, cut them into smaller pieces. This recipe is designed for a 6-quart Instant Pot®. If you have an 8-quart model, then you can put 12 cups (3 liters) of water and a few extra vegetables and an extra onion into the pot and make more stock. With all stocks, feel free to let the pot remain on warm for longer, even a few hours, if that works best with your schedule.

Press the Sauté button until the medium button lights up. When the display reads "Hot," add the oil, onions, leeks, and garlic. Cook for 5 minutes, stirring often. Add the water and use a wooden spoon to scrape the bottom of the pot clean. Press Cancel.

Add the carrots, celery, parsnips, fennel, squash, mushrooms, peppercorns, mustard seeds, coriander seeds, turmeric, salt, black and white pepper, and parsley.

Secure the lid, ensuring that the steam release handle is in the Sealing position. Press the Pressure Cook button and set the cooking time for 35 minutes. When the cooking time is complete, let the pot sit to naturally release the pressure for 10 minutes. Turn the steam release handle to the Venting position to release any remaining pressure. Press Cancel and remove the lid. Strain the stock through a fine mesh sieve, pressing the vegetables to get as much flavor as possible into the stock.

GLUTEN-FREE, PARVE, PASSOVER (WITHOUT MUSTARD SEEDS), VEGAN

HANDS-ON TIME: 9 Minutes

TIME TO PRESSURE: 33 Minutes

COOKING TIME: 35 Minutes

BUTTONS TO USE: Sauté and Pressure Cook

RELEASE TYPE: Natural Release for 10 Minutes

ADVANCE PREP: May be made 4 days in advance or frozen

Makes 13 cups (about 3 liters)

2 tablespoons oil

3 medium onions, halved and sliced

2 leeks, white and light green only, sliced

1 head garlic, cloves separated, 2 cloves peeled and chopped

8 cups (2 liters) water, or 12 cups (3 liters) if using an 8-quart device

4 carrots, peeled and cut into thirds

4 stalks celery, cut into thirds

2 parsnips, peeled and cut into thirds

1 fennel, quartered

1 cup (80g) butternut squash cubes

ingredients continue on the following page

FREEZING STOCK

To have stock on hand for other recipes, after you have cooled the soup, transfer into containers, 2 or 4 cups (473ml or 1 liter) at a time. Label with a permenent marker on masking tape the amount in the container so you can thaw as needed.

CLEANING LEEKS

Leeks are generally filthy, so you need to clean them very carefully. First trim the end off the white part, and then cut off the dark green part, and discard both. You can even do this when you return from the store so the leeks take up less storage space in your fridge. Slice the leek lengthwise and discard the two outermost layers. Slice through another few layers, but not all the way through. Under running water, fan open the leek layers and rinse off between the layers, checking for dirt or sand. If you find a lot of dirt, then cut deeper into the leek and rinse well. You can also slice the leeks as directed in a recipe, soak the pieces in water in a salad spinner, and then drain.

1 cup (80g) sliced shiitake mushrooms

1 tablespoon black peppercorns

1 tablespoon yellow mustard seeds

1 tablespoon coriander seeds

1 teaspoon turmeric

½ teaspoon kosher salt

¼ teaspoon black pepper

pinch white pepper

handful of Italian parsley leaves and stems

BEEF BONE BROTH
(page 49)

VEGETABLE STOCK
(page 44)

CLASSIC CHICKEN SOUP WITH HERBED MATZOH BALLS

This was one of those IP® recipes I was nervous to try after seeing so many people post online that you needed to cook it for hours to get enough flavor in the soup. The first time I made this, I cooked it for 45 minutes and then did natural release for 2 hours, because I left the house to do errands. I returned to soup with a deep flavor. For an 8-quart IP®, you can use more celery and 2 to 3 more cups of water.

Place the chicken pieces into the inner pot. Add the onions, carrots, celery, garlic, ginger, parsnip, fennel, mushrooms, parsley, dill, bay leaves, salt, peppercorns, mustard seeds, fennel seeds, cumin seeds, and water.

Secure the lid, ensuring that the steam release handle is in the Sealing position. Press the Pressure Cook button and set the cooking time for 45 minutes.

To make the matzoh balls, place the eggs, oil, herbs, salt, pepper, and seltzer into a large bowl and whisk together. Add the matzoh meal and whisk well. Cover loosely with plastic and place into the fridge for at least 1 hour. Wet your hands and shape into balls about 1½ inches (4cm) diameter and place onto a plate.

When the soup cooking time is complete, let the pot sit to naturally release the pressure for 30 minutes and as long as

MEAT, PASSOVER
(WITHOUT MUSTARD SEEDS)

SOUP

HANDS-ON TIME:	12 Minutes
TIME TO PRESSURE:	30–33 Minutes
COOKING TIME:	45 Minutes, plus 5 Minutes on Warm
BUTTONS TO USE:	Sauté and Pressure Cook
RELEASE TYPE:	Natural Release for 30 Minutes to 2 hours
ADVANCE PREP:	May be made 3 days in advance or frozen

MATZOH BALLS

TIME TO PRESSURE:	8 Minutes
COOKING TIME:	15 Minutes
BUTTON TO USE:	Pressure Cook
RELEASE TYPE:	Natural Release for 10 Minutes
ADVANCE PREP:	Batter may be made 1 day in advance

Serves 8–10
Makes 10 ¾ cups (2.5 liters) soup

SOUP

1 whole chicken, cut into quarters

1 large onion, quartered

2 carrots, peeled and cut into quarters

2 stalks celery, cut in half crosswise

ingredients continue on the following page

2 hours. Turn the steam release handle to the Venting position. Press Cancel and open the lid. Let cool. Taste the soup and add more salt or pepper if necessary. Strain through a large sieve into a large container or other pot. Let cool.

If you are saving the soup as stock, place into containers in two-, four-, or six-cup (473ml, 1 liter, or 1.5 liters) amounts and label to use or freeze.

If serving as soup, strain the soup. Separate out 3 cups (710ml) of soup and set aside. Press Sauté to bring the soup to a boil. Add the matzoh balls and press Cancel. Secure the lid, ensuring that the steam release handle is in the Sealing position. Press the Pressure Cook button and set the cooking time for 15 minutes. When the cooking is complete, allow the pot to sit for 10 minutes to naturally release the pressure. Turn the steam release handle to the Venting position to release any additional pressure. Press Cancel and remove the lid. Return the reserved soup to the pot and press Warm to warm the soup. Serve the soup with the matzoh balls.

4 cloves garlic, peeled

2-inch (5cm) chunk of fresh ginger

2 parsnips, peeled and cut in half

1 fennel bulb, quartered

½ cup (40g) sliced shiitake mushrooms, about 4 large

1 cup (25g) Italian parsley leaves

1 cup (25g) fresh dill

2 bay leaves

1 teaspoon kosher salt

1 tablespoon black peppercorns

1 teaspoon mustard seeds

½ teaspoon fennel seeds

½ teaspoon cumin seeds

7 cups (1.7 liters) water or to the maximum fill line

MATZOH BALLS

4 large eggs

3 tablespoons oil

2 tablespoons chopped herbs, such as a combination of parsley, thyme, and dill

1½ teaspoons kosher salt

pinch white pepper

⅓ cup (79ml) seltzer

1 cup (127g) matzoh meal

BEEF BONE BROTH

While researching healthy foods I came across information suggesting that bone broth had magical properties. It is believed to boost your immune system because it improves gut health. It has collagen, which helps your joints and is good for your skin. Bone broth is rich in minerals such as iron, calcium, and magnesium. The longer it cooks, the more nutrients it has, so this is a good recipe to make in the morning and then let sit and warm for a long while. The vinegar helps draw the nutrients out of the bones. You can drink it daily like taking a vitamin or turn it into a soup and serve it with any leftover meat or chicken, vegetables, and some rice noodles.

Set the oven to broil and place the meat bones into a roasting pan. Broil for 10 minutes, using tongs to turn them over after 5 minutes. Place into the inner pot along with the flanken, carrots, celery, parsnip, onion, garlic, ginger, bay leaf, thyme, vinegar, salt, pepper, and water.

Secure the lid, ensuring that the steam release handle is in the Sealing position. Press the Pressure Cook button and set the cooking time for 120 minutes. When the cooking time is complete, let the pot sit to naturally release the pressure for 60 minutes or up to 3 hours. Turn the steam release handle to the Venting position. Press Cancel and remove the lid.

Strain the broth, using a cheesecloth draped over a strainer, making sure to catch any small bone pieces.

MEAT, PASSOVER

HANDS-ON TIME:	14 Minutes
TIME TO PRESSURE:	14 Minutes
COOKING TIME:	10 Minutes to broil bones, then 120 Minutes in IP®
BUTTON TO USE:	Pressure Cook
RELEASE TYPE:	Natural Release for 60 Minutes to 3 hours
ADVANCE PREP:	May be made 3 days in advance or frozen

Makes 9 cups (2.25 liters) broth, serves 6–8 as a soup

3 pounds (1.3kg) beef marrow bones

1½ pounds (680g) flanken, cut into 3-inch (7.5cm) pieces

2 carrots, peeled and cut into 1-inch (2.5cm) pieces

3 stalks celery, cut into 1-inch (2.5cm) pieces

1 parsnip, peeled and cut into 1-inch (2.5cm) pieces

1 large onion, cut into 1-inch (2.5cm) pieces

3 cloves garlic, peeled

1-inch (2.5cm) piece of fresh ginger

1 dried bay leaf

3 sprigs thyme

ingredients continue on the following page

If you are serving as a soup rather than a broth, separate the flanken meat and shred it. Add to the soup along with any of the garnishes.

WHAT'S A SOUP SOCK

You can use a "soup sock," a mesh bag to hold soup ingredients so that they can be easily lifted out of the soup when it is cooked. In this recipe use one to hold the flanken and beef bones and a second to hold the vegetables. Do your best to squeeze out as much liquid from the bone and vegetable bags as you can.

---

1 tablespoon apple cider vinegar

$\frac{1}{2}$ teaspoon kosher salt

$\frac{1}{2}$ teaspoon black pepper

8 cups (2 liters) water

SOUP GARNISH

cooked rice noodles

shredded cooked chicken (see page 80)

shredded leftover meat

shredded carrots

bean sprouts

cilantro leaves

leftover cooked broccoli

INDIAN SPICED CARROT SOUP

Back when I was a young lawyer working at a law firm, before I ever imagined that food was a possible career path, I used to cook soups like this one, freeze servings in gallon freezer bags, and then bring them to work and reheat them for lunch.

Press Sauté, and when the display reads "Hot," add the oil, onions, ginger, and garlic to the inner pot and cook for 5 minutes. Stir occasionally. Add the curry powder and turmeric and cook for 2 minutes. Press Cancel.

Add the stock and use a wooden spoon to scrape the bottom of the pot clean. Add the carrots, peanut butter, salt, and pepper and stir.

Secure the lid, ensuring that the steam release handle is in the Sealing position. Press the Pressure Cook button and set the cooking time for 5 minutes. When the cooking time is complete, turn the steam release handle to the Venting position to quickly release the pressure.

Press Cancel and remove the lid. Use an immersion blender to purée the soup for 3 full minutes. Taste and add more salt and pepper as needed.

SOUP PURÉES

Whenever you are puréeing a soup, be sure to purée for at least 3 full minutes so that the soup is velvety smooth.

GLUTEN-FREE, MEAT OR PARVE, PASSOVER, VEGAN
(WITH VEGETABLE STOCK)

HANDS-ON TIME:	11 Minutes
TIME TO PRESSURE:	10 Minutes
COOKING TIME:	5 Minutes
BUTTONS TO USE:	Sauté and Pressure Cook
RELEASE TYPE:	Quick Release
ADVANCE PREP:	May be made 3 days in advance or frozen

Serves 6–8 people

2 tablespoons oil

2 large onions, chopped into ½-inch (1.5cm) pieces

2½ tablespoons chopped fresh ginger

4 cloves garlic, roughly chopped

2 teaspoons curry powder

1 teaspoon turmeric

6 cups (1.5 liters) chicken stock or Vegetable Stock (see pages 44 and 47)

2 pounds (907g) carrots, peeled and sliced into ½-inch (1.2cm) slices

1 tablespoon natural peanut butter (or almond or sunflower butter)

½ teaspoon salt

¼ teaspoon white pepper

GOLDEN TOMATO SOUP

GLUTEN-FREE, PARVE,
PASSOVER, VEGAN

HANDS-ON TIME: 11 Minutes

TIME TO PRESSURE: 24 Minutes

COOKING TIME: 5 Minutes

BUTTONS TO USE: Sauté and Pressure
Cook

RELEASE TYPE: Quick Release

ADVANCE PREP: May be made 3 days
in advance or frozen

Serves 8–10

I had originally intended to serve this soup cold, but one time I tasted it hot and decided it was just as good warm, so the temperature is up to you. It is a very pretty yellow color and would look great in small cups served at a party.

Press Sauté and when the display reads "Hot," add the oil, shallots, onions, celery, carrots, and 4 of the chopped garlic cloves to the inner pot. Cook for 4 minutes, stirring a few times. Add the yellow cherry tomatoes, yellow peppers, turmeric, water, salt, and white pepper, and stir, scraping the bottom clean.

Secure the lid, ensuring that the steam release handle is in the Sealing position. Press the Pressure Cook button and set the cooking time for 5 minutes. When the cooking time is complete, turn the steam release handle to the Venting position to quickly release the pressure. Remove the lid and add the large yellow tomatoes and remaining chopped garlic. Press Cancel. Use an immersion blender to purée the tomatoes until the soup is very smooth, for at least 3 minutes. Strain if desired. Taste for salt or pepper and add more if needed.

Serve hot or chill for 4 hours or overnight. Ladle into bowls and add garnish as desired.

¼ cup (59ml) extra virgin olive oil

2 large shallots, halved and sliced

2 medium onions, sliced

2 stalks celery, chopped into
1-inch (1.5cm) pieces

2 carrots, sliced

6 cloves garlic, roughly chopped,
divided

20 ounces (567g) yellow cherry
tomatoes; you can use some light
red ones as well

3 yellow peppers, cut into 2-inch
(5cm) chunks

1 teaspoon turmeric

5 cups (1.25 liters) water

½ teaspoon salt

pinch white pepper

*ingredients continue
on the following page*

4 large yellow tomatoes, seeds removed, and cut into 2-inch (5cm) pieces

sliced cherry or grape tomatoes of any color

cilantro

avocado cubes

SUPERGREEN SOUP

This is basically a soup with a pile of nutritious green vegetables thrown in. To avoid the usual dull green color of green vegetable soups, I add spinach only at the end and purée when it is just wilted.

GLUTEN-FREE, PARVE, PASSOVER (WITHOUT PEAS)

HANDS-ON TIME:	15 Minutes
TIME TO PRESSURE:	13 Minutes
COOKING TIME:	5 Minutes plus 2 Minutes to steam spinach
RELEASE TYPE:	Quick Release
BUTTONS TO USE:	Sauté and Pressure Cook
ADVANCE PREP:	May be made 3 days in advance or frozen

Serves 10–12

Press Sauté and when the display reads "Hot," add the oil, leeks, onions, celery, and garlic to the inner pot and cook for 5 to 6 minutes, stirring occasionally, or until the onions look clear. Add the turmeric, garlic powder, onion powder, salt, white pepper, and thyme, and cook for another 1½ minutes, stirring often. Add the water and use a wooden spoon to scrape the bottom of the pot clean. Add the zucchini, broccoli, and peas and stir. Press Cancel.

Secure the lid, ensuring that the steam release handle is in the Sealing position. Press the Pressure Cook button and set the cooking time for 5 minutes. When the cooking time is complete, turn the steam release handle to the Venting position to quickly release the pressure.

Leave the IP® on Warm. Remove the lid and add the spinach and basil. Use a wooden spoon to press them into the soup. Secure the lid and let sit on the Warm setting for 2 minutes. Remove the lid and use an immersion blender to purée for three full minutes. Press Cancel. Add the honey

3 tablespoons extra virgin olive oil

2 leeks, white and light green parts only, halved lengthwise and sliced

2 large onions, halved and sliced

1 stalk celery, chopped into ½-inch (1.2cm) pieces

6 cloves garlic, roughly chopped

1½ teaspoons turmeric

1½ teaspoons garlic powder

1½ teaspoons onion powder

1½ teaspoons kosher salt

⅛ teaspoon white pepper

1 teaspoon dried thyme

5 cups (1.25 liters) water

ingredients continue on the following page

and a generous grinding of black pepper. Taste and add more salt as needed.

To serve, ladle into bowls, drizzle with olive oil, and sprinkle some pine nuts on top.

1 pound (454g) zucchini, cut into 1-inch (2.5cm) pieces

1½ pounds (680g) broccoli, florets chopped into 1½-inch (4cm) pieces and stems into 1-inch (2.5cm) pieces

½ cup (75g) frozen peas

about 7 cups (210g) baby spinach leaves

10 large basil leaves (.75 ounce [27g] box)

1 tablespoon honey

freshly ground black pepper

high-quality olive oil to drizzle on top

toasted pine nuts for garnish (see page 160)

EVERYDAY VEGETABLE SOUP

Most of my soup recipes came about by serendipity. I simply opened my fridge and took whatever vegetables were around and created soup out of them. In every instance I would sauté onions or leeks with garlic in oil and then chop up the lonely vegetables, throw them in, add whatever spices fancied me, and then cover them with stock or water. Over time, my kids would ask for certain of my made-up recipes, so finally I was forced to write them down. I still make clean-out-the-fridge soups every time I return home from a trip.

Press Sauté and when the display reads "Hot," add the oil, onions, celery, carrots, bay leaves, and sage to the inner pot and cook for 6 minutes, or until the onions start to color. Add the garlic and 3 tablespoons of the parsley and cook for 1 minute. Add the stock, tomato paste, farro, salt, and pepper. Press Cancel.

Secure the lid, ensuring that the steam release handle is in the Sealing position. Press the Pressure Cook button and set the cooking time for 16 minutes. When the cooking time is complete, turn the steam release handle to the Venting position to quickly release the pressure.

Add the zucchini, corn kernels, and kidney beans and stir. Secure the lid, ensuring that the steam release handle is in the Sealing position. Press the Pressure Cook button and set the cooking time for 2 minutes. When the cooking time is

GLUTEN-FREE, MEAT OR PARVE (DEPENDING ON THE STOCK), **VEGAN** (WITH VEGETABLE STOCK)

HANDS-ON TIME:	13 Minutes
PREP TIME:	10 Minutes
TIME TO PRESSURE:	21 Minutes
COOKING TIME:	16 Minutes, plus 2 Minutes at the end
BUTTONS TO USE:	Sauté and Pressure Cook
RELEASE TYPE:	Quick Release
ADVANCE PREP:	May be made 3 days in advance or frozen

Serves 10

2 tablespoons extra virgin olive oil

1 large red onion, chopped into ½-inch (1.2cm) pieces

2 stalks celery, chopped into ½-inch (1.2cm) pieces

2 carrots, peeled and diced into ½-inch (1.2cm) pieces

2 bay leaves

10 sage leaves, chopped

2 cloves garlic, minced

¼ cup (6g) chopped Italian parsley leaves, divided

9 cups (2.2 liters) chicken stock or Vegetable Stock (see pages 44 and 47)

ingredients continue on the following page

complete, turn the steam release handle to the Venting position to quickly release the pressure. Press Cancel and remove the lid.

Add the remaining parsley, more salt and pepper as needed, and serve.

1 tablespoon tomato paste (see tip, page 74)

1 cup (200g) farro

½ teaspoon salt

¼ teaspoon black pepper

1 large zucchini, cut into ¾-inch (2cm) cubes

Corn kernels, from 2 ears of fresh corn

1 (15-ounce [425g]) can red kidney beans, drained and rinsed

BORSCHT

GLUTEN-FREE, PARVE, PASSOVER, VEGAN

HANDS-ON TIME: **7 Minutes**

TIME TO PRESSURE: **17 Minutes**

COOKING TIME: **10 Minutes**

BUTTONS TO USE: **Sauté and Pressure Cook**

RELEASE TYPE: **Quick Release**

ADVANCE PREP: **May be made 3 days in advance or frozen**

This is an old-world Jewish classic made hip again because everyone now recognizes the health benefits of beets. Serve hot or cold.

Press Sauté and when the display reads "Hot," add the oil and onions to the inner pot and cook for 3 minutes, stirring occasionally. Add the beets, water or stock, carrot, parsnip, potatoes, lemon juice, dill, salt, and pepper and stir.

Secure the lid, ensuring that the steam release handle is in the Sealing position. Press the Pressure Cook button and set the cooking time for 10 minutes. When the cooking time is complete, turn the steam release handle to the Venting position to quickly release the pressure. Press Cancel and remove the lid. Use an immersion blender to purée for 4 full minutes.

Serves 10–12

2 tablespoons oil

1 large onion, cut into ½-inch (1.2cm) pieces

3 large beets, peeled and cut into 1-inch (2.5cm) pieces

6 cups (1.5 liters) water or Vegetable Stock (see page 44)

1 carrot, peeled and cut into 1-inch (2.5cm) pieces

1 parsnip, peeled and cut into chunks

2 medium potatoes, peeled and cut into 2-inch (5cm) chunks

2 tablespoons fresh lemon juice, from 1 large lemon

1 cup (10g) fresh dill

1 teaspoon salt

⅛ teaspoon white pepper

MUSHROOM BARLEY SOUP

The first soup I ever made in my life was the mushroom barley soup from the famous *Moosewood Cookbook*. Moosewood was also the first cookbook I ever purchased when I had my first apartment in law school. Inspired by that recipe, I have always added soy sauce to my own versions of this soup. For a soy-free soup, use red wine instead.

Press Sauté and when the display reads "Hot," add 2 tablespoons of the oil and onions to the inner pot and cook for 4 minutes, stirring occasionally. Add the remaining oil, white mushrooms, shiitake mushrooms, and garlic and cook for 3 minutes, stirring often. Add the stock, barley, salt, and pepper and stir, scraping the bottom clean. Press Cancel.

Secure, the lid, ensuring that the steam release handle is in the Sealing position. Press the Pressure Cook button and set the cooking time for 18 minutes. When the cooking time is complete, let sit for 10 minutes to naturally release the pressure. Turn the steam release handle to the Venting position to release any remaining pressure.

Add the soy sauce and dill, and cover. Let sit on Warm for 5 minutes. Add more salt and pepper as needed.

GLUTEN-FREE, PARVE, VEGAN

HANDS-ON TIME:	12 Minutes
TIME TO PRESSURE:	12 Minutes
COOKING TIME:	18 Minutes
BUTTONS TO USE:	Sauté and Pressure Cook
RELEASE TYPE:	Natural Release for 10 Minutes, then Warm for 5 Minutes
ADVANCE PREP:	May be made 3 days in advance or frozen

Serves 8–10

3 tablespoons oil, divided

2 large onions, chopped into ½-inch (1.2cm) pieces

1 pound (454g) white mushrooms, sliced

3 ounces (85g) shiitake mushrooms, sliced

4 cloves garlic, finely chopped

8 cups (2 liters) Vegetable Stock (see page 44)

¾ cup (150g) pearled barley

½ teaspoon salt

½ teaspoon black pepper

2 tablespoons soy sauce

2 tablespoons chopped fresh dill

BUTTERNUT SQUASH SOUP

GLUTEN-FREE, PARVE,
PASSOVER, VEGAN

HANDS-ON TIME:	13 Minutes
TIME TO PRESSURE:	6 Minutes
COOKING TIME:	10 Minutes
BUTTONS TO USE:	Sauté and Pressure Cook
RELEASE TYPE:	Quick Release
ADVANCE PREP:	May be made 3 days in advance or frozen

Serves 10–12

I was pretty excited when boxes of cubed butternut squash appeared in supermarkets because it really is a time saver. Unfortunately, the quality and freshness varied greatly and the cubes often spoiled before I could use them. I went back to buying whole squash and peeling, seeding, and cubing it myself and discovered the taste was dramatically better. This soup is thick, so add water as needed when reheating.

2 tablespoons oil

2 large onions, sliced

1 shallot, sliced

3 cloves garlic, roughly chopped

2 tablespoons chopped fresh ginger

½ teaspoon ground cinnamon

½ teaspoon salt

2 pinches white pepper

6 cups (1.5 liters) Vegetable Stock (see page 44), divided

4 pounds (1.7kg) butternut squash, peeled and cubed, see below

2 medium apples, peeled, cored, and quartered

Press Sauté and when the display reads "Hot," add the oil, onions, shallots, garlic, and ginger to the inner pot and cook for 3 minutes, stirring often. Add the cinnamon, salt, and pepper and stir. Add 2 cups (473ml) of the stock and use a wooden spoon to scrape the bottom of the pot clean. Press Cancel. Add the remaining stock, squash, and apples and stir.

Secure the lid, ensuring that the steam release handle is in the Sealing position. Press the Pressure Cook button and set the cooking time for 10 minutes. When the cooking time is complete, turn the steam release handle to the Venting position to quickly release the pressure. Press Cancel and remove the lid. Use an immersion blender to purée for 4 full minutes. Add more salt and white pepper as needed.

If serving the next day, add ½ cup (118ml) of water or more to thin out the soup.

CUTTING SQUASH CUBES

Use a vegetable peeler to peel the squash and remove as much peel as possible. Cut off the ends and then slice into 1½-inch (4cm) discs. Remove the seeds and cut the slices into cubes.

OLD WORLD BEEF AND BARLEY SOUP

This is an official family recipe and one of the staples of the Shoyer home. The recipe comes from the Marcus (paternal) side of my family, and it has nourished my children from their first teeth. It is a meal in a bowl and the ultimate comfort food. It is best made the day before so you can remove the fat on top of the soup before eating.

Press Sauté and when the display reads "Hot," add the oil, onions, carrots, celery, leeks, and garlic to the inner pot and cook for 5 minutes, stirring occasionally. Add 2 cups of the water, stir, and scrape the bottom clean. Add the meat, drained lima beans, barley, remaining water, half of the dill, half of the parsley, salt, and pepper and stir. Press Cancel.

Secure the lid, ensuring that the steam release handle is in the Sealing position. Press the Pressure Cook button and set the cooking time for 35 minutes. When the cooking time is complete, turn the steam release handle to the Venting position to quickly release the pressure. Press Cancel and remove the lid.

Add the remaining dill and parsley and stir. Remove the meat from the pot and cut into smaller chunks between the bones and return to the pot. Add more salt and pepper if needed.

HANDS-ON TIME:	8 Minutes, soak lima beans for at least 1 hour or overnight
TIME TO PRESSURE:	12 Minutes
COOKING TIME:	35 Minutes
BUTTONS TO USE:	Sauté and Pressure Cook
RELEASE TYPE:	Quick Release
ADVANCED PREP:	May be made 3 days in advance or frozen

Serves 10

3 tablespoons oil

1 large onion, chopped into ½-inch (1.2cm) pieces

3 carrots, peeled and chopped into ½-inch (1.2cm) pieces

4 celery stalks, chopped into ½-inch (1.2cm) pieces

2 leeks, white and light green only, quartered the long way and sliced

4 cloves garlic, finely chopped

11 cups (2.7 liters) water, divided

1½ pounds (680g) top rib meat/flanken, cut into large pieces between the bones

½ cup (100g) small lima beans, soaked overnight or for 1 hour in hot water

1 cup (200g) pearled barley

ingredients continue on the following page

2 tablespoons chopped fresh dill, divided

1 tablespoon chopped curly parsley, divided

1 teaspoon kosher salt, or more to taste

½ teaspoon black pepper, or more to taste

LENTIL AND SQUASH SOUP

This recipe idea is attributed to Judith Gold, who was emptying her freezer and removed two small mysterious containers: one with squash soup and another with lentil soup. She decided to combine them in one soup pot, and when she raved about the results, I decided to try this recipe. Then I researched lentil and squash soup recipes and learned that they already existed. It is a very thick and filling soup.

Press Sauté and when the display reads "Hot," add the oil, onions, celery, carrots, and garlic to the inner pot and cook for 3 minutes, stirring occasionally. Add the turmeric, cumin, salt, and pepper and cook for 1 minute. Add the stock and use a wooden spoon to scrape the bottom of the pot clean. Add the tomatoes and juice, lentils, sweet potato, and squash and stir. Press Cancel.

Secure the lid, ensuring that the steam release handle is in the Sealing position. Press the Pressure Cook button and set the cooking time for 10 minutes. When the cooking time is complete, turn the steam release handle to the Venting position to quickly release the pressure. Press Cancel and remove the lid. Stir. Let the device stay on Warm.

Use an immersion blender to partially purée the soup for 8 to 10 seconds. Add the spinach or kale leaves and stir. Secure the lid without turning the valve to the Sealing position. Let it sit on Warm for 5 minutes. Stir and serve.

GLUTEN-FREE, PARVE, VEGAN

HANDS-ON TIME:	10 Minutes
TIME TO PRESSURE:	25 Minutes
COOKING TIME:	10 Minutes Minutes, plus 5 Minutes on Warm
BUTTONS TO USE:	Sauté and Pressure Cook
RELEASE TYPE:	Quick Release
ADVANCE PREP:	May be made 3 days in advance or frozen

Serves 10

2 tablespoons extra virgin olive oil

2 onions, chopped into ½-inch (1.2cm) pieces

2 stalks celery, cut into ½-inch (1.2cm) pieces

2 carrots, cut into ½-inch (1.2cm) pieces

4 cloves garlic, roughly chopped

1 teaspoon turmeric

1½ teaspoons cumin

½ teaspoon salt

½ teaspoon black pepper

6 cups (1.5 liters) Vegetable Stock (see page 44)

⅔ cup (340g) canned diced tomatoes and juice

ingredients continue on the following page

1½ (288g) cups brown lentils

1 large sweet potato, about
1 pound (454g), peeled and cut
into 1½-inch (4cm) chunks

2 cups (680g) butternut squash
cubes

2 cups (680g) baby spinach or
kale leaves

POTATO LEEK SOUP

My late father, Reubin Marcus, *z"l*, was a huge fan of any kind of soup, but potato leek soup was one of his favorites of my recipes. You can make it dairy with half and half or parve with cashew cream, which is a great cream substitute and so easy to make.

If making the cashew cream, about 5 hours before you want to cook the soup, place the cashews into a bowl and cover with 1 cup (236ml) of the water. Let sit.

Press Sauté and when the display reads "Hot," add the oil, onions, and leeks to the inner pot and cook until they look clear, stirring often, for about 7 minutes. Add the garlic and cook for 1 minute. Add 2 cups (473ml) of the stock and cook for 1 minute, scraping the bottom of the pot clean. Add the potatoes, remaining stock, thyme, garlic powder, salt, and pepper and stir. Press Cancel.

Secure the lid, ensuring that the steam release handle is in the Sealing position. Press the Pressure Cook button and set the cooking time for 10 minutes.

If making the cashew cream, while the soup is cooking, drain the cashews and place into the bowl of a food processor. Add the remaining 1 cup (473ml) of cold water and process until very creamy, for about 2 minutes.

GLUTEN-FREE, DAIRY OR PARVE,
PASSOVER, VEGAN

HANDS-ON TIME:	Soak cashews for 5 hours, 18 Minutes prep
TIME TO PRESSURE:	21 Minutes
COOKING TIME:	10 Minutes
BUTTONS TO USE:	Sauté and Pressure Cook
RELEASE TYPE:	Quick Release
ADVANCE PREP:	May be made 3 days in advance or frozen

Serves 8–10

SOUP

3 tablespoons extra virgin olive oil

1 large onion, chopped into ½-inch (1.2cm) pieces

6 leeks, white and light green parts, halved lengthwise, rinsed well and sliced into 1-inch (2.5cm) pieces; quarter lengthwise if 2-inch (5cm) thick (see page 45 for cleaning leeks)

6 cloves garlic, finely chopped

7 cups (1.7 liters) Vegetable Stock (see page 44), divided

4 medium potatoes, peeled and cut into ½-inch (1.2cm) cubes

½ teaspoon fresh thyme leaves

½ teaspoon garlic powder

¾ teaspoon salt

*ingredients continue
on the following page*

When the cooking time is complete, turn the steam release handle to the Venting position to quickly release the pressure. Remove the lid. Use an immersion blender to purée for just a few seconds. Add the half and half or cashew cream and press Warm until serving.

¾ teaspoon black pepper

½ cup (118ml) half and half or cashew cream, see below

CASHEW CREAM

1 cup (138g) raw cashews

2 cups (473ml) cold water, divided

FRENCH ONION SOUP PURÉE WITH SHREDDED SHORT RIBS

GLUTEN-FREE, MEAT, PASSOVER

HANDS-ON TIME: 35 Minutes

TIME TO PRESSURE: 13 Minutes

COOKING TIME: 30 Minutes

BUTTONS TO USE: Sauté and Pressure Cook

RELEASE TYPE: Quick Release

ADVANCE PREP: May be made 3 days in advance or frozen

Serves 6–8

French onion soup is perfect on a cold winter day. Adding shredded short ribs or flanken turns it into a meal. Be careful to make sure that there are no bones in the pot before you purée the soup.

4 tablespoons oil, divided

2 strips short rib/flanken on the bone, about 1½ pounds (680g) total, each strip cut in half

4 large onions, about 2½ pounds (1kg) total, sliced, 12 cups (3 liters) sliced

5 cloves garlic, roughly chopped

3 cups (710ml) hot water

1 teaspoon salt

1 teaspoon black pepper

5 sprigs fresh thyme

Press Sauté, making sure the time is set for 30 minutes, and when the displays reads "Hot," add 2 tablespoons of the oil to the inner pot. Add the meat and sear for 3 minutes on each side, or until browned. Remove to a plate and set aside.

Add the remaining oil and the onions, and use long tongs to stir. Cook for 25 minutes total time, stirring about every 4 minutes.

After the onions have cooked for about 15 minutes, use a wooden spoon to scrape the bottom of the pot to mix around the browned pieces into the other onions. If the machine goes off, turn it back on to Sauté.

Add the garlic and cook for another 2 minutes. Add the water and stir for a minute with a wooden spoon, scraping the bottom of the pot clean again. Press Cancel. Add the salt, pepper, and thyme. Return the meat to the pot.

Secure the lid, ensuring that the steam release handle is in the Sealing position. Press the Pressure Cook button and set the

HARIRA SOUP

GLUTEN-FREE
(WITH SUBSTITUTION), **MEAT**

HANDS-ON TIME: Soak chickpeas the
night before,
35 Minutes prep

TIME TO PRESSURE: 17 Minutes for soup,
5 Minutes for rice

COOKING TIME: 20 Minutes for soup,
5 more Minutes for
rice

BUTTONS TO USE: Sauté and Pressure
Cook

RELEASE TYPE: Quick Release

ADVANCE PREP: May be made 3 days
in advance or frozen

Serves 8–10

Our December 2018 family trip to Morocco was, according to my children, more of a road trip than a vacation, as we traveled from Casablanca to Marrakesh to the Sahara, up to Fez with side trips to Essaouira and Chefchauen, and hiking in the Atlas Mountains. We found Jewish history all over the country. We ate a vegetarian version of this soup one morning for breakfast. It is the official soup eaten to end the Ramadan fast day, but it really is a meal in a bowl. I learned from journalist David Suissa that his Moroccan family eats harira after the Yom Kippur fast. For a gluten-free version, substitute cornstarch for the flour.

Place the onions, celery, carrots, and garlic into the bowl of a food processor and pulse to chop the vegetables into very small pieces. Press Sauté and when the display reads "Hot," add the oil and chopped vegetables to the inner pot and cook for 5 minutes. Meanwhile, place the parsley into the processor bowl and chop fine. Remove to a bowl. Add the cilantro to the processor bowl and chop into small pieces. Remove to a separate bowl. Add the canned tomatoes with juice and the tomato paste to the processor. Purée completely. Set aside in the processor bowl.

After the vegetables have cooked, add the meat, cumin, cinnamon, ginger, turmeric, paprika, fine salt, and pepper and stir to distribute. Cook for 2 minutes, stirring occasionally. Drain the chickpeas and add to the pot along with the lentils, parsley, tomato purée, and 6 cups (1.5 liters) of the water. Stir and scrape the bottom clean. Press Cancel.

1 onion, quartered

3 stalks celery, each cut into quarters

2 carrots, peeled and cut into 2-inch (5cm) chunks

3 cloves garlic, peeled

3 tablespoons extra virgin olive oil

1 cup (25g) Italian parsley leaves

1 cup (25g) cilantro leaves, divided

1 (14.5-ounce [428ml]) can of whole or diced tomatoes with juice

2 tablespoons tomato paste

½ pound (227g) pepper steak or other beef stew meat, cut into ¾- to 1-inch (2cm to 2.5cm) cubes

ingredients continue on the following page

Secure the lid, ensuring that the steam release handle is in the Sealing position. Press the Pressure Cook button and set the cooking time for 20 minutes. In the meantime, mix together the flour and remaining ¼ cup (59ml) water in a small bowl.

When the cooking time is complete, turn the steam release handle to the Venting position to quickly release the pressure. Press Cancel and remove the lid.

Use a wooden spoon to stir the soup very well and make sure nothing is stuck to the bottom of the pot. Add half of the cilantro, the rice, kosher salt, and the flour and water mixture. Stir. Secure the lid, ensuring that the steam release handle is in the Sealing position. Press the Pressure Cook button and set the cooking time for 5 minutes. When the cooking time is complete, turn the steam release handle to the Venting position to quickly release the pressure. Press Cancel and remove the lid.

Stir in the lemon juice and serve. Serve garnished with the remaining cilantro.

1 teaspoon cumin

1 teaspoon cinnamon

2 teaspoons ground ginger

1 teaspoon turmeric

1 teaspoon paprika

2 teaspoons fine salt

1 teaspoon black pepper

⅓ cup (70g) chickpeas soaked in 2 cups (473ml) water overnight

¼ cup (50g) lentils

6 cups (1.5 liters) water, plus ¼ cup (59ml), divided

2 tablespoons flour (or cornstarch)

⅓ cup (65g) rice (can use brown rice if desired)

¼ teaspoon kosher salt

1 tablespoon lemon juice, from 1 lemon

FREEZING TOMATO PASTE

After you have opened a can of tomato paste and used some, take out a tablespoon measuring spoon. Scoop up 1 tablespoon at a time of tomato paste and wrap each one in plastic wrap. When done, place all of the wrapped pieces into a plastic bag and freeze. You can take out what you need each time and it will not go bad in the fridge.

PERUVIAN CHICKEN SOUP (AGUADITO)

GLUTEN-FREE, MEAT

HANDS-ON TIME:	9 Minutes
TIME TO PRESSURE:	19 Minutes
COOKING TIME:	5 Minutes
BUTTONS TO USE:	Sauté and Pressure Cook
RELEASE TYPE:	Quick Release
ADVANCE PREP:	May be made 2 days in advance

Serves 8

I make the Whole Roasted Peruvian Chicken on page 80 for dinner a day or two before I want to make this soup, eat half of the chicken for dinner, and save the other half for the soup. You can also buy a rotisserie chicken for it to save time.

Press Sauté and when the display reads "Hot," add the oil, onions, Poblano pepper, jalapeño, 2 halved green onions, and garlic to the inner pot and cook for 4 minutes, stirring often; you do not want the onions to brown. Transfer into the bowl of a food processor or blender and set aside. Add ½ cup (118ml) hot water to the inner pot and bring to a boil. Use a wooden spoon to scrape the bottom of the pot clean. Press Cancel.

Place the chicken stock, remaining water, potatoes, carrots, celery, rice, peas, and cumin into the pot. Secure the lid, ensuring that the steam release handle is in the Sealing position. Press the Pressure Cook button and set the cooking time for 5 minutes. When the cooking time is complete, turn the steam release handle to the Venting position to quickly release the pressure. Press Cancel and remove the lid.

Place a sieve over a bowl and scoop up about 1 cup of the soup from the pot and pour over the strainer into the bowl. Return the solids in the sieve to the pot. Add the strained stock to the food processor bowl. Add salt and pepper to taste, half of the

2 tablespoons oil

1 medium onion, chopped into ½-inch (1.2cm) pieces

1 large Poblano pepper, chopped into 2-inch (5cm) pieces

1 jalapeño pepper, seeds removed and roughly chopped

4 green onions, divided, 2 halved across and 2 sliced for garnish

4 cloves garlic, chopped

1½ cups (354ml) hot water, divided

5½ cups (1.3 liters) chicken stock (see page 47)

1 medium Yukon gold potato, chopped into 1-inch pieces

2 carrots, peeled and diced into small cubes

1 stalk celery, cut into small cubes

ingredients continue on page 77

cilantro leaves, and the lime juice and then purée completely. Add the remaining cilantro and purée.

Pour the green purée back into the pot along with the shredded chicken. Add the remaining green onions. If eating immediately, replace the cover, press Warm, and let warm until serving, at least 10 minutes. If reheating later, let the soup cool and then place into a container to refrigerate.

$\frac{1}{3}$ cup (65g) rice

$\frac{1}{2}$ cup (65g) frozen peas

1 teaspoon cumin

$\frac{1}{2}$ teaspoon salt

black pepper to taste

1 bunch cilantro leaves

2 tablespoons lime juice from 2 limes

2 cups shredded chicken, about half of a small chicken

SEEDING JALAPEÑO PEPPERS

First put on gloves. Trim the end off of the jalapeño and then slice in half lengthwise. Use a 1/2-teaspoon measuring spoon to scoop out the seeds into the garbage. This works best with a metal measuring spoon.

MEAT MAINS

Whole Peruvian Spiced Chicken — 80

Hungarian Chicken Paprikash — 83

Orange Chicken — 85

Coq au Vin — 88

Chicken Shwarma with Avocado Tahini — 90

Pulled Chicken Tacos in Mole Sauce — 92

Veal Osso Buco — 94

Veal Stew with Mushrooms and Orange — 96

Turkey for Four — 97

Jewish Meets Irish Corned Beef and Potatoes — 98

Roast Beef with Rosemary and Wine Sauce — 100

Grandma's Stuffed Cabbage — 101

Bertha's Meatballs — 104

Meatloaf Packed with Vegetables — 106

Spaghetti with Flanken Bolognese — 108

Cholent with a Twist — 110

Texas Chili — 112

Spinach Pesto Brisket — 115

Persian Lamb and Herb Stew — 117

Marrakesh Beef Tagine with Prunes and Peanuts — 118

Spicy Ribs with Coffee and Chili Sauce — 121

WHOLE PERUVIAN SPICED CHICKEN

This super-easy spice combination is easy to double or triple and have on hand for chicken, steak, or fish. The mix of spices comes from our wonderful nanny, Betty Supo. She is from Arequipa, Peru, and has nourished our family for many years.

In a small bowl, combine the cumin, paprika, garlic powder, salt, and pepper. Drizzle 1 tablespoon of the oil over the chicken and rub to coat. Shake the spice mixture onto the chicken and rub all over.

Press Sauté and when the display reads "Hot," add the remaining oil. Place the chicken into the inner pot, breast-side down, and cook for 4 minutes, or until browned. Turn over and brown for another 4 minutes. Remove the chicken to a plate.

Add the boiling water to the pot and use a wooden spoon to scrape the bottom of the pot clean. Place the steam rack into the pot, and place the chicken on the rack, breast-side up. Secure the lid, ensuring that the steam release handle is in the Sealing position. Press the Pressure Cook button and set the cooking time for 25 minutes.

When the cooking time is complete, let the pot sit for another 15 minutes to naturally release the pressure. Turn the steam release handle to the Venting position to release any remaining pressure. Press Cancel.

GLUTEN-FREE, MEAT, PASSOVER

HANDS-ON TIME: 17 Minutes

TIME TO PRESSURE: 10 Minutes

COOKING TIME: 25 Minutes

RELEASE TYPE: Natural Release for 15 Minutes

BUTTONS TO USE: Sauté and Pressure Cook

ADVANCE PREP: May be made 2 days in advance

Serves 4–6

4 teaspoons cumin

1 tablespoon paprika

2 teaspoons garlic powder

¼ teaspoon salt

¼ teaspoon black pepper

2 tablespoons extra virgin olive oil, divided

1 whole chicken, about 3–4 pounds (1.3–2kg)

1 cup (236ml) boiling water

1 tablespoon cornstarch or potato starch, optional

Remove the lid, take out the chicken, and place onto a serving platter. Press Sauté and cook the drippings for 4 minutes or more, to reduce the sauce. To thicken the sauce further, you can scoop up about ¼ cup (59ml) of the drippings into a small bowl, add the cornstarch, and mix, and return to the pot and stir.

Cut the chicken into serving pieces. Pour some sauce over the chicken and serve the remaining sauce in a bowl alongside. If you make this the day before you are serving it, you can remove the fat from the reserved sauce before reheating.

SPICE BLENDS AS GIFTS

If you have a favorite combination of spices, such as this one, you can make a larger batch and place in a jar to give as a host or hostess or holiday gift. Make sure to include on the label how many chickens you can make with the amount gifted.

HUNGARIAN CHICKEN PAPRIKASH

GLUTEN-FREE, MEAT, PASSOVER

HANDS-ON TIME:	5 hours to soak the cashews, 40 Minutes prep
TIME TO PRESSURE:	25 Minutes
COOKING TIME:	14 Minutes
BUTTONS TO USE:	Sauté and Pressure Cook
RELEASE TYPE:	Quick Release
ADVANCE PREP:	May be made 2 days in advance, cashew cream may be made 1 day in advance

Serves: 8–10

Although my maternal grandmother's family was Hungarian, I never tried this wonderful chicken dish until I was an adult. The classic recipe is made with sour cream, but I use a homemade cashew cream instead. If you want to skip that step, use the canned thick coconut cream. This recipe yields a lot of sauce so serve with farfalle pasta or use quinoa when you serve it on Passover.

About 5 hours before you want to cook the chicken, place the cashews into a bowl and cover with 1 cup (236ml) of the water. Let sit.

Press Sauté and make sure the time is set for 30 minutes. When the display reads "Hot," add the oil to the inner pot. Brown the chicken in batches, about 4 pieces at a time and about 4 minutes per side, until well-browned. Transfer to a large pan. Add the onions and garlic and cook for 3 minutes, stirring often. Add the paprika, Aleppo pepper, and smoked paprika and cook for 30 seconds, stirring almost the entire time. Add the stock and use a wooden spoon to scrape the bottom of the pot clean. Add the tomatoes and stir. Return the chicken to the pot, placing the dark meat pieces on the bottom and the white meat pieces on top.

Secure the lid, ensuring that the steam release handle is in the Sealing position. Press the Pressure Cook button and set the cooking time for 14 minutes.

CHICKEN

2 tablespoons oil

2 medium-size chickens, each cut into eight pieces

1 large onion, chopped into ½-inch (1.2cm) pieces

4 cloves garlic, roughly chopped

¼ cup Hungarian paprika

¼ teaspoon Aleppo pepper or black pepper

pinch smoked paprika

2 cups (473ml) chicken stock (see page 47)

1 cup (242g) crushed tomatoes

CASHEW CREAM

1 cup (137g) raw cashews

2 cups (473ml) water, divided

While the chicken is cooking, drain the cashews and place into the bowl of a food processor. Add the remaining 1 cup of water and process until very creamy, for about 2 full minutes, scraping down the bowl as needed. Set aside.

When the cooking time is complete, turn the steam release handle to the Venting position to quickly release the pressure. Press Cancel and remove the lid.

Remove the chicken to a serving platter and press Sauté. Cook the sauce for 5 minutes to reduce and thicken, stirring occasionally. Add the cashew cream and cook for 1 minute. Pour over the chicken.

IP° CHICKEN TIP

When cooking chicken pieces in the IP®, always place the dark meat pieces on the bottom and the white meat pieces on top so that the white pieces, which take less time to cook, do not become dry.

ORANGE CHICKEN

GLUTEN-FREE, MEAT

HANDS-ON TIME:	20 Minutes
PREP TIME:	10 Minutes
TIME TO PRESSURE:	13 Minutes
COOKING TIME:	12 Minutes
BUTTONS TO USE:	Sauté and Pressure Cook
RELEASE TYPE:	Quick Release
ADVANCE PREP:	May be made 2 days in advance

I happened to buy blood oranges by accident the first time I made this chicken, but it is just as good with navel oranges. You can also buy an extra blood orange to garnish the serving platter, as the color is so vibrant.

Serves 4–6

Press Sauté and when the display reads "Hot," add the oil and 3 or 4 pieces of chicken to the inner pot. Brown for about 3 to 4 minutes per side, until golden. Remove to a plate.

Meanwhile, in a bowl or measuring cup, place the orange zest and juice, ginger, garlic, brown sugar, wine, Sriracha, soy sauce, sesame oil, honey, salt, and pepper and whisk well. Brown the second batch of chicken as you did the first. Remove to the plate.

Add the water to the pot and use a wooden spoon to scrape the bottom of the pot clean. Press Cancel. Return the chicken to the pot, first the dark meat pieces and then the white meat pieces on top. Pour the sauce over the chicken.

Secure the lid, ensuring that the steam release handle is in the Sealing position. Press the Pressure Cook button and set the cooking time for 12 minutes. When the cooking time is complete, turn the steam release handle to the Venting position to quickly release the pressure. Press Cancel and remove the lid.

Remove the chicken to a serving platter. Press Sauté. Scoop up ½ cup (118ml) of the sauce and place into a small bowl. Add

1 tablespoon oil

1 chicken, cut into 8 pieces

1 tablespoon zest of 1 blood or navel orange

1 cup (236ml) fresh orange juice, from 3–4 blood or navel oranges

1½ tablespoons chopped fresh ginger; from a 3-inch (7.5cm) long chunk

6 cloves garlic, crushed

¼ cup (55g) light brown sugar

2 tablespoons white wine or white grape juice

2 teaspoons Sriracha or other hot sauce

2 tablespoons soy sauce

1 teaspoon toasted sesame oil

1 tablespoon honey

ingredients continue on the following page

the cornstarch, mix well, and return to the pot. Cook for 4 to 5 minutes to thicken the sauce. Taste for salt and pepper and add more if needed. Pour the sauce over the chicken and serve.

¼ teaspoon salt

¼ teaspoon black pepper

½ cup (118ml) water

3 tablespoons cornstarch

FREEZING FRESH GINGER

Fresh ginger root can be peeled and kept in the freezer until you need it. The freezing makes it easier to chop and grate it as well.

CHICKEN SHWARMA WITH AVOCADO TAHINI

Serve the chicken and avocado tahini with pita, Israeli salad, and Hummus (see page 29). It is also great on top of salad greens.

Rub 1 tablespoon of the oil, ¼ cup (25g) of the shwarma spice, and the turmeric all over the chicken and let marinate in the fridge for 15 minutes to 1 hour. Place the stock into the inner pot and add the chicken pieces.

Secure the lid, ensuring that the steam release handle is in the Sealing position. Press the Pressure Cook button and set the cooking time for 10 minutes. When the cooking time is complete, turn the steam release handle to the Venting position to quickly release the pressure. Press Cancel and remove the lid.

Strain the chicken, reserving ½ cup (118ml) of the liquid. Wipe out the pot with paper towels and press Sauté. When the display reads "Hot," add the remaining oil, onions, and garlic and cook for 6 to 8 minutes, stirring occasionally and making sure they do not burn.

Meanwhile, use two forks to break up the chicken into long pieces, but do not completely shred it. Add it to the pot along with another teaspoon of the shwarma spice, salt, pepper, and ¼ cup (59ml) of the chicken cooking liquid. Cook for 3 minutes, stirring often. If the texture becomes too dry, add an

GLUTEN-FREE, MEAT, PASSOVER (WITHOUT TAHINI)

HANDS-ON TIME: Marinate chicken for 15 Minutes before cooking, 15 Minutes prep

TIME TO PRESSURE: 9 Minutes

COOKING TIME: 10 Minutes

BUTTONS TO USE: Sauté and Pressure Cook

RELEASE TYPE: Quick Release

ADVANCE PREP: Chicken may be made 2 days in advance

Serves 6–8

CHICKEN

2 tablespoons extra virgin olive oil, divided

¼ cup (25g) shwarma spice mix, plus 1 teaspoon, divided

1 teaspoon turmeric

2 pounds (907g) dark meat boneless chicken (*pargiyot*)

1 cup (236ml) chicken stock or Vegetable Stock (see pages 44 and 47)

1 large onion, chopped into ½-inch (1.2cm) pieces

2 cloves garlic, roughly chopped

½ teaspoon kosher salt

½ teaspoon black pepper

ingredients continue on the following page

additional tablespoon or more of the chicken cooking liquid. Add more salt or pepper to taste.

To prepare the tahini, place the garlic into the bowl of the food processor and chop into small pieces. Add the tahini, avocado, lemon juice, and water and process, scraping down the bowl a few times. Add the oil, salt, and pepper, adding more if necessary to taste, and process until creamy. If the mixture is too thick, add a tablespoon or more of ice water and process again. Serve with the chicken.

AVOCADO TAHINI

1 clove garlic

½ cup (120g) tahini

1 ripe avocado

2 tablespoons fresh lemon juice, from 1–2 lemons

¼ cup (59ml) ice water, or more to make it creamy

2 tablespoons extra virgin olive oil

¼ teaspoon salt

¼ teaspoon black pepper

PULLED CHICKEN TACOS IN MOLE SAUCE

GLUTEN-FREE, MEAT, PASSOVER

HANDS-ON TIME:	15 Minutes
TIME TO PRESSURE:	16 Minutes
COOKING TIME:	6 Minutes
BUTTONS TO USE:	Sauté and Pressure Cook
RELEASE TYPE:	Natural Release for 7 Minutes
ADVANCE PREP:	Chicken may be made 2 days in advance or frozen

When my kids were young, I discovered that they were most excited about those meals they could assemble themselves at the table. You can serve this chicken in a flour or corn tortilla or create a taco bowl with rice, lettuce, and avocado and pour extra sauce on top.

Serves 6

Press Sauté and when the display reads "Hot," add the oil, onions, and garlic to the inner pot. Cook for 3 minutes, stirring occasionally. Add the stock, tomatoes, chopped chile and soaking liquid, cocoa, cinnamon, coriander, cloves, salt, and pepper and cook for 3 minutes. Press Cancel.

Use an immersion blender to purée the sauce, or transfer to a food processor or blender and then return to the pot. Add the chicken and turn to coat.

Secure the lid, ensuring that the steam release handle is in the Sealing position. Press the Pressure Cook button and set the cooking time for 6 minutes. When the cooking time is complete, let the pot sit for 7 minutes to naturally release the pressure. Turn the steam release handle to the Venting position to release any remaining pressure. Press Cancel and remove the lid.

Remove the chicken and use two forks to shred into strips. Meanwhile, press Sauté and cook the sauce for 4 minutes to thicken.

2 tablespoons oil

2 large onions, chopped into ½-inch (1.2cm) pieces

3 cloves garlic, roughly chopped

1 cup (236ml) chicken stock or Vegetable Stock (see pages 44 and 47)

2 tomatoes, seeded and cut into 1-inch (2.5cm) pieces

1 dried ancho chile, soaked in ¾ cup (177ml) hot water, then chopped

2 tablespoons unsweetened cocoa

¼ teaspoon cinnamon

¼ teaspoon coriander

¼ teaspoon cloves

¼ teaspoon salt

ingredients continue on the following page

Place the chicken pieces into a serving bowl and pour some sauce on top. Serve in a tortilla or as a taco bowl with rice, sliced avocado, salsa, or any other toppings.

¼ teaspoon black pepper

6 boneless chicken breasts, about 3 pounds (1.3kg) total

FOR SERVING:

tortillas

sliced avocado

shredded lettuce

white or brown rice

salsa

VEAL OSSO BUCO

GLUTEN-FREE, MEAT, PASSOVER

HANDS-ON TIME:	36 Minutes
TIME TO PRESSURE:	29 Minutes
COOKING TIME:	35 Minutes
BUTTONS TO USE:	Sauté and Pressure Cook
RELEASE TYPE:	Quick Release
ADVANCE PREP:	May be made 2 days in advance

Serves 6–8

Osso buco is an Italian cut of veal shanks, round with a bone in the center. This recipe is from Valerie Lack, an Italian-American-Jewish friend I met in Geneva, Switzerland, and it remains one of my all-time favorite dishes. It typically cooks for at least two hours, so the IP® is a real time saver.

¼ cup (28g) all-purpose flour or potato starch

8 medium veal shanks

¼ cup (59ml) extra virgin olive oil, plus 1 tablespoon, divided

2 large onions, halved and sliced

2 carrots, peeled and thinly sliced into rounds

2 stalks celery, thinly sliced

2 bay leaves

½ cup (118ml) white wine

1 (28-ounce [828ml]) can crushed tomatoes

2 tablespoons tomato paste

½ teaspoon salt

¼ teaspoon black pepper

1 cup (236ml) hot water

2 tablespoons finely chopped fresh parsley

4 cloves garlic, crushed

1 tablespoon lemon zest, from 1 lemon

Press Sauté, making sure the time is set for 30 minutes. Place the flour on a plate and dip in the veal pieces to dust with the flour. Shake off the excess flour. When the display reads "Hot," add ¼ cup of the oil to the inner pot and brown the veal shanks in batches, about 3 to 4 minutes per side, and remove to a plate once the pieces have some crispy parts. Add another tablespoon of oil along with the onions, carrots, celery, and bay leaves and cook, using a wooden spoon to scrape up any pieces of meat that are stuck to the bottom of the pot. Cook until the onions are translucent, about 3 minutes, scraping the bottom of the pan a few times.

Add the wine and cook for 3 minutes, stirring often. Add the tomatoes and fill half the tomato can with water and add to the pot along with the tomato paste and bring to a boil. Add the salt and pepper and stir. Remove the sauce to a large bowl. Add the water to the inner pot and use a wooden spoon to scrape the bottom of the pan clean. Press Cancel.

Place the steam rack inside the inner pot. Place one layer of the veal pieces on top of the rack, some of the sauce, another layer of meat, and alternate until all the meat is inside. Pour any remaining sauce on top.

Secure the lid, ensuring that the steam release handle is in the Sealing position. Press the Pressure Cook button and set the cooking time for 35 minutes.

While the veal is cooking, prepare the gremolata. Combine the parsley, garlic, and lemon zest in a small bowl. When the cooking time is complete, turn the steam release handle to the Venting position to quickly release the pressure. Press Cancel and remove the lid. Place the osso buco and sauce into a large serving bowl. Sprinkle the gremolata over the meat and sauce, pressing some into the sauce.

VEAL STEW WITH MUSHROOMS AND ORANGE

Every cook can remember the first cookbooks they ever loved. One of mine was *The New Basics* by Sheila Lukins and Julee Rosso. I still have my original copy with half the pages falling out from overuse. This recipe is inspired by their Veal and Mushroom Stew.

Press Sauté and when the display reads "Hot," add 2 tablespoons of the oil and half of the veal cubes to the inner pot. Cook for 4 to 5 minutes, turning every minute, until browned on all sides. Remove to a bowl. Add another 2 tablespoons of oil and brown the second batch. Remove to the bowl. Carefully lift the inner pot and pour any liquid over the veal in the bowl.

Add the remaining 2 tablespoons of oil and mushrooms. Cook for 2 minutes, stirring occasionally. In a small bowl, mix the paprika, coriander, pepper, and flour and add to the mushrooms. Cook for 30 seconds, stirring the entire time. Add the wine and stock and cook for 1 minute, scraping the bottom of the pan clean. Add the tomatoes, shallots, garlic, orange zest, and salt and stir. Return the veal to the pot and stir.

Secure the lid, ensuring that the steam release handle is in the Sealing position. Press the Pressure Cook button and set the cooking time for 25 minutes. When the cooking time is complete, turn the steam release handle to the Venting position to quickly release the pressure. Press Cancel and remove the lid. Stir. Press Sauté and cook to thicken the sauce for 5 minutes, stirring occasionally. Add the orange juice and stir. Serve garnished with chopped parsley.

GLUTEN-FREE, MEAT, PASSOVER (WITH POTATO STARCH)

HANDS-ON TIME: 22 Minutes

TIME TO PRESSURE: 12 Minutes

COOKING TIME: 25 Minutes

RELEASE TYPE: Quick Release

BUTTONS TO USE: Sauté and Pressure Cook

ADVANCE PREP: May be made 2 days in advance or frozen

Serves 6–8

6 tablespoons oil, divided

2 pounds (907g) veal cubes, no larger than 1½ inch (4cm)

16 ounces (454g) white mushrooms, halved and large ones quartered

1 tablespoon paprika

2 teaspoons coriander

½ teaspoon black pepper

2 tablespoons all-purpose flour, cornstarch, or potato starch

½ cup (118ml) white wine

½ cup (118ml) chicken stock

1 (28-ounce [828ml]) can crushed tomatoes

10 shallots, peeled

4 cloves garlic, roughly chopped

2 teaspoons orange zest, from 1 large orange (reserve juice)

½ teaspoon salt

3 tablespoons orange juice, from zested orange

⅓ cup (8g) Italian parsley leaves, chopped, for garnish

TURKEY FOR FOUR

Turkey is too good to serve only once a year, so occasionally I buy a breast or parts and roast them for Shabbat or a weeknight dinner. The IP® makes the turkey meat super moist, and you can broil the pieces at the end if you want a crispy skin.

Press Sauté and when the display reads "Hot," add the oil. Brown the turkey legs for 4 minutes per side, or until browned. Remove to a plate. Add the thighs, skin side down, and brown for 4 minutes. Turn over and cook for another 2 minutes. Remove to the plate. While the turkey is browning, chop the rosemary, sage, and thyme leaves into small pieces. Set aside.

Add the onions and shallots to the pot and cook for 2 minutes, stirring often. Add the wine and use a wooden spoon to scrape the bottom of the pot clean. Add the stock and chopped herbs and stir. Return the turkey pieces to the pan.

Secure the lid, ensuring that the steam release handle is in the Sealing position. Press the Pressure Cook button and set the cooking time for 35 minutes. When the cooking time is complete, turn the steam release handle to the Venting position to quickly release the pressure. Press Cancel and remove the lid.

Remove the turkey pieces to a roasting pan. Broil for 3 minutes, if desired.

Press Sauté and cook the drippings for 3 minutes. Place the cornstarch into a small bowl. Scoop up ½ cup (118ml) of the drippings into the bowl and whisk to dissolve. Return to the pot and cook for 2 minutes. Strain and serve.

GLUTEN-FREE, MEAT, PASSOVER (WITH POTATO STARCH)

HANDS-ON TIME: 25 Minutes

TIME TO PRESSURE: 10 Minutes

COOKING TIME: 35 Minutes

BUTTONS TO USE: Sauté and Pressure Cook

RELEASE TYPE: Quick Release

ADVANCE PREP: May be made 2 days in advance or frozen

Serves 4

2 tablespoons extra virgin olive oil

2 turkey legs

2 turkey thighs

leaves of 2 sprigs rosemary

8 sage leaves

1 teaspoon thyme leaves

1 large onion, chopped into ½-inch (1.2cm) pieces

2 shallots, sliced

½ cup (118ml) white wine

1 cup (236ml) chicken stock or Vegetable Stock (see pages 44 and 47)

2 tablespoons cornstarch or potato starch

Serve with Cranberry and Orange Sauce (page 169).

JEWISH MEETS IRISH CORNED BEEF AND POTATOES

GLUTEN-FREE, MEAT, PASSOVER (WITH WINE, NOT BEER)

HANDS-ON TIME: 2 Minutes

TIME TO PRESSURE: 18 Minutes

COOKING TIME: 90 Minutes, plus 10 Minutes for the potatoes

BUTTON TO USE: Pressure Cook

RELEASE TYPE: Quick Release

ADVANCE PREP: May be made 2 days in advance

Serves 6

I grew up eating corned beef at Long Island kosher delis and didn't know that people ate it warm until I studied at the London School of Economics and had Shabbat meals with families in the London Jewish community. The Brits call it salt beef and serve it with potatoes. I decided to go full-on Irish with beer but I omitted the cabbage because it just isn't tasty enough. You can also skip the potatoes and just cook the meat to serve cold in sandwiches, or my favorite way: on top of a mountain of arugula and sliced avocado, drizzled with balsamic vinegar and oil.

1 (3–4-pound [1.3–2kg]) corned beef brisket

3 cloves garlic

3 tablespoons pickling spices

1 teaspoon dried thyme

2 cups (473ml) water

2 cups (473ml) dark beer or white wine

1 pound (454g) small round potatoes

Rinse off the spices that come with the meat, if packaged that way. Place the garlic, pickling spices, thyme, and water into the inner pot. Place the steam rack. Place the meat on top of the rack and pour the beer over it.

Secure the lid, ensuring that the steam release handle is in the Sealing position. Press the Pressure Cook button and set the cooking time for 90 minutes. When the cooking time is complete, turn the steam release handle to the Venting position to quickly release the pressure. Press Cancel and remove the lid.

Remove the meat to a platter, pour a ladleful of the liquid over it, and cover with foil to keep warm.

Place the potatoes on top of the steam rack. Secure the lid, ensuring that the steam release handle is in the Sealing position. Press the Pressure Cook button and set the cooking time for 10 minutes. When the cooking time is complete, turn the steam release handle to the Venting position to quickly release the pressure. Press Cancel and remove the lid.

Slice the meat and serve with the potatoes and good-quality grainy mustard.

ROAST BEEF WITH ROSEMARY AND WINE SAUCE

The IP® is a good choice for many types of meat because the meat becomes very tender in a short amount of time and the inner pot is much easier to clean than a roasting pan. I serve this with my Cranberry and Orange Sauce, see page 169.

Press Sauté and when the display reads "Hot," add the oil to the inner pot along with the meat. Cook until browned on all sides, about 2 to 3 minutes per side, for 10 to 12 minutes total. Remove to a plate.

Add the shallots and onions and cook for 3 minutes, stirring often. Add the wine and use a wooden spoon to scrape the bottom clean. Cook for 4 minutes, stirring often. Press Cancel. Add the stock, water, rosemary, garlic powder, paprika, salt, and pepper and stir. Return the meat to the pot.

Secure the lid, ensuring that the steam release handle is in the Sealing position. Press the Pressure Cook button and set the cooking time for 60 minutes. When the cooking time is complete, let the pot sit for 10 minutes to naturally release the pressure. Turn the valve to the Venting position to release any remaining pressure. Press Cancel and remove the lid.

Remove the meat to a cutting board and cover with foil. Press Sauté and cook the sauce for 4 minutes to thicken. Slice the meat and place on a platter. Strain the gravy into a boat and pour some over the meat.

GLUTEN-FREE, MEAT, PASSOVER

HANDS-ON TIME:	25 Minutes
TIME TO PRESSURE:	6 Minutes
COOKING TIME:	60 Minutes
RELEASE TYPE:	Natural Release for 10 Minutes
BUTTONS TO USE:	Sauté and Pressure Cook
ADVANCE PREP:	May be made 2 days in advance or frozen

Serves 6

2 tablespoons oil

4 pounds (2kg) chuck eye roast

3 shallots, sliced

1 onion, cut into ½-inch (1.2cm) pieces

1 cup (236ml) red wine

1 cup (236ml) Beef Bone Broth (see page 49) or chicken stock or Vegetable Stock (see pages 44 and 47)

2 cups (473ml) hot water

1 sprig rosemary

1 teaspoon garlic powder

1 teaspoon paprika

¼ teaspoon salt

½ teaspoon black pepper

GRANDMA'S STUFFED CABBAGE

GLUTEN-FREE, MEAT

HANDS-ON TIME:	45 Minutes
TIME TO PRESSURE:	25 Minutes
COOKING TIME:	18 Minutes
BUTTONS TO USE:	Sauté and Pressure Cook
RELEASE TYPE:	Natural Release for 15 Minutes
ADVANCE PREP:	May be made 2 days in advance or frozen

Makes 16 cabbage rolls

The credit for this recipe goes to my grandma Sylvia Altman, *z"l*, even though I have made some changes to it over the years. Her original recipe used every saucepan in my kitchen, and I have shifted to napa rather than green cabbage, as it is easier to roll. She would never have believed that you could have melt-in-your-mouth stuffed cabbage cooked without watching the rolls cook for hours.

Cut off the end of the cabbage and separate 17 leaves. Bring a medium or large saucepan of water to a boil on the stovetop. Place a colander over a bowl near the saucepan. Cook the leaves, about 6 at a time, for 4 minutes per batch, leaving the water boiling the entire time. Use tongs to lift the cooked leaves and place into the colander to drain. Try not to tear the leaves. Place on paper towels or a clean dishtowel to dry.

To make the sauce, press Sauté and when the display reads "Hot," add the oil, chopped onions, and apples. Cook for about 5 minutes, until they start to soften but not brown, stirring often.

Prepare the cabbage filling. Finely chop the onion by hand or in a food processor. Place into a large bowl. Add the beef, rice, egg, ¼ cup (59 ml) water, salt, and pepper, and mix well with your hands. Fan out a cabbage leaf in front of you with the stem facing you. Scoop up a handful of the meat and rice mixture, about ¼ cup for each roll, and place at the bottom of a cabbage leaf, at the stem.

CABBAGE ROLLS

1 head napa cabbage

1 onion

1 pound ground beef

⅓ cup (65g) white rice

1 large egg

¼ cup (59ml) water

½ teaspoon salt

¼ teaspoon black pepper

SAUCE

1 tablespoon oil

2 medium onions, chopped into small dice

1 large green apple, peeled and cut into ¾-inch (2cm) cubes

1 (28-ounce [828ml]) can crushed tomatoes

ingredients continue on page 103

Fold the bottom over the mixture and roll over again, and then fold the sides of the leaf toward the middle to cover the meat, and then roll up.

When the onions and apples are cooked, add the crushed tomatoes, 1 cup (236 ml) water, lemon juice, brown sugar, and honey and bring to a boil. Add salt and black pepper.

Remove sauce to a large bowl. Add ½ cup (118ml) hot water to the inner pot and boil, and use a wooden spoon to scrape the bottom of the pot clean. Place the steam rack on top. Place one layer of rolls on the rack, one ladle of sauce, another layer of rolls, and so on, pouring any remaining sauce on top. Sprinkle the golden raisins on top.

Secure the lid, ensuring that the steam release handle is in the Sealing position. Press the Pressure Cook button and set the cooking time for 18 minutes. When the cooking time is complete, let the pot sit for 15 minutes to naturally release the pressure. Turn the valve to the Venting position to release any remaining pressure. Press Cancel and remove the lid. If you like a thicker sauce, remove the cabbage rolls to a serving bowl, press Sauté, and cook the sauce down for 5 minutes, stirring often, until the desired thickness is achieved.

1½ cups (354ml) water, divided

¼ cup (59ml) fresh lemon juice, from 1–2 lemons

5 tablespoons (60g) light brown sugar

1 tablespoon honey

½ teaspoon salt

¼ teaspoon black pepper

⅓ cup (50g) golden raisins

BERTHA'S MEATBALLS

As of the writing of this book, Bertha Glickman is 101 years old. I received this meatball recipe from her daughter Suzin, *z"l*, who passed away at age 53 in January 2015, the same week her father also died, at age 98. Bertha is remarkably strong and sharp. After one bite of these meatballs maybe 20 years ago, I was converted to Bertha's recipe.

To make the meatballs, place the egg, breadcrumbs, ½ cup (59ml) of the crushed tomatoes, oregano, salt, and pepper into a bowl and whisk well. Add the meat and use your hands to knead the mixture together for a few minutes. Form meatballs, about 1½ inches (4cm) in diameter, and place on a plate.

To make the sauce, press Sauté and when the display reads "Hot," add the olive oil, onions, and garlic and cook for 3 minutes, stirring occasionally. Add 1 cup (236 ml) of the water, remaining crushed tomatoes, tomato paste, basil, thyme, oregano, sugar, salt, and pepper. Cook for 1 minute. Press Cancel.

Secure the lid, ensuring that the steam release handle is in the Sealing position. Press the Pressure Cook button and set the cooking time for 8 minutes. When the cooking time is complete, let the pot sit for 10 minutes to naturally release the pressure. Turn the steam release handle to the Venting position to release any remaining pressure. Press Cancel and remove the lid.

MEAT

HANDS-ON TIME:	10 Minutes
TIME TO PRESSURE:	18 Minutes
COOKING TIME:	8 Minutes for sauce, 8 Minutes for meatballs
BUTTONS TO USE:	Sauté and Pressure Cook
RELEASE TYPE:	Natural Release for 10 Minutes for sauce, Quick Release for meatballs
ADVANCE PREP:	May be made 3 days in advance or frozen

Serves 6, 14 meatballs

MEATBALLS

1 large egg

½ cup (60g) seasoned Italian-flavored breadcrumbs

½ cup (59ml) crushed tomatoes, from the 28-ounce (828ml) can you need for the sauce

¼ teaspoon oregano

⅛ teaspoon salt

¼ teaspoon black pepper

1 pound (454g) ground meat

ingredients continue on the following page

Scoop up 2 cups (473ml) of the sauce and remove to a large serving bowl. Keep warm. Add 1½ cups (354ml) of water to the sauce. Add the meatballs to the sauce. Secure the lid, ensuring that the steam release handle is in the Sealing position. Press the Pressure Cook button and set the cooking time for 8 minutes. When the cooking time is complete, turn the steam release handle to the Venting position to quickly release the pressure. Press Cancel and remove the lid.

Add the reserved sauce to the pot and stir gently. Serve with your favorite pasta.

SAUCE

1 tablespoon extra virgin olive oil

1 small onion, chopped into ¼-inch (6mm) pieces

3 cloves garlic, roughly chopped

2½ cups (591ml) water, divided

1 (28-ounce [828ml]) can crushed tomatoes

1 (14.5-ounce [428ml]) can crushed tomatoes

2 tablespoons tomato paste

¼ teaspoon dried basil

¼ teaspoon thyme

¼ teaspoon oregano

2 teaspoons sugar

½ teaspoon salt

½ teaspoon black pepper

MEATLOAF PACKED WITH VEGETABLES

MEAT

HANDS-ON TIME: 30 Minutes

TIME TO PRESSURE: 7 Minutes

COOKING TIME: 35 Minutes

BUTTONS TO USE: Sauté and Pressure Cook

RELEASE TYPE: Natural Release for 10 Minutes

ADVANCE PREP: May be made 2 days in advance or frozen

Serves 6

When my kids were little, I used to make this meatloaf on a regular basis, and my daughter Emily would help me. Over time, my four children preferred meatballs and spaghetti, and so this recipe was put on the back burner. Cooking it in the IP® yields a very moist texture and then broiling it at the end gives you the perfect crunch on top.

Place the onions, carrots, celery, garlic, green onions, and red pepper into the bowl of a food processor fitted with a metal blade. Pulse to chop into small pieces, and be careful to not purée. Press Sauté and when the display reads "Hot," add the oil and chopped vegetables to the inner pot and cook until soft, for about 10 minutes, stirring occasionally. Press Cancel.

Meanwhile, in a large bowl place the tomato sauce, eggs, cumin, salt, black pepper, red pepper, white pepper, and nutmeg, and whisk until combined. Add the meat and breadcrumbs and mix well with your hands.

Place the vegetables into a bowl and use a silicone spatula to press the vegetables up the sides of the bowl to cool them faster. Place that bowl into a larger bowl containing ice cubes and water. Let sit for 10 minutes, stirring a few times, to cool the vegetables quickly.

1 large onion, halved and each half cut into thirds

1 carrot, peeled and cut into 2-inch (5cm) chunks

1 stalk celery, cut into quarters

2 cloves garlic, peeled

1 green onion, cut into thirds

1 red pepper, cut into 2-inch (5cm) chunks

2 tablespoons extra virgin olive oil

⅓ cup (83ml) tomato sauce

2 large eggs

½ teaspoon cumin

¼ teaspoon salt

⅛ teaspoon black pepper

pinch red pepper

pinch white pepper

ingredients continue on the following page

Add the cooled vegetables to the meat mixture and knead by hand for a few minutes to distribute all the vegetables.

Take a large piece of heavy-duty aluminum foil, about 15 × 15 inches (38 × 38cm), fold in half and then in half again to shape it into a square, and then fold up the edges about 1 inch (2.5cm) to create a boat. Shape the meat into a round or oval loaf and place it onto the foil. Add the 1 cup of water to the inner pot. Carefully place the foil and meatloaf on top of the steam rack and then lift and lower the rack into the inner pot.

Secure the lid, ensuring that the steam release handle is in the Sealing position. Press the Pressure Cook button and set the cooking time for 35 minutes. When the cooking time is complete, let sit for 10 minutes to naturally release the pressure. Turn the steam release handle to the Venting position to release any remaining pressure. Set your oven to broil. Press Cancel and remove the lid.

Tilt the foil to drain any excess liquid around the meatloaf into the pot. Lift up the rack and loaf to a baking pan and slide the foil and meatloaf onto the pan. Set the steam rack aside.

Brush the top with the barbeque sauce and broil the loaf for 7 to 10 minutes, until browned, watching carefully so that it does not burn.

pinch nutmeg

1 pound (454g) ground beef

½ cup (60g) flavored breadcrumbs

1 cup (236ml) water

¼ cup (59ml) barbeque sauce

SPAGHETTI WITH FLANKEN BOLOGNESE

This book was nearly complete when I saw how excited people were about versions of spaghetti Bolognese in the IP®. To give it my own Jewish spin, I added flanken meat along with the ground beef. Flanken is a cut of ribs that has been cut across the bone into strips. It is commonly used in cholent as well as Korean short rib recipes. It adds texture to the sauce.

Press Sauté and when the display reads "Hot," add 2 tablespoons of the oil, onions, and garlic to the inner pot. Cook for 3 minutes, stirring occasionally. Add the ground beef and flanken and cook to brown the meat for 5 minutes, pressing the meat pieces into the bottom of the pan, and stirring occasionally to brown on all sides. Add the wine and cook for 3 minutes to cook off some of the wine. Add the pepper. Press Cancel.

Grab half of the spaghetti and break the strands in half. Rinse under cold water and place each handful into the pot with the strands going in different directions. Repeat for the remaining spaghetti. Drizzle the remaining oil on top of the spaghetti strands. Pour the sauce over the pasta. Fill the jar with water and pour over the pasta. Add some salt on top. Do not stir.

Secure the lid, ensuring that the steam release handle is in the Sealing position. Press the Pressure Cook button and set the cooking time for 15 minutes.

MEAT

HANDS-ON TIME:	21 Minutes
TIME TO PRESSURE:	15 Minutes
COOKING TIME:	15 Minutes
BUTTONS TO USE:	Sauté and Pressure Cook
RELEASE TYPE:	Quick Release
ADVANCE PREP:	May be made 2 days in advance

Serves 6

3 tablespoons extra virgin olive oil, divided

1 medium onion, chopped into ½-inch (1.2cm) pieces

4 cloves garlic, roughly chopped

1 pound (454g) ground beef

½ pound (227g) deboned flanken or short ribs, cut into ⅓-inch (8mm) pieces

½ cup (118ml) white wine

¼ teaspoon black pepper

1 pound (454g) uncooked spaghetti

24 ounces (710ml) marinara sauce

water to fill the sauce jar

salt to taste

black pepper to taste

When the cooking time is complete, turn the steam release handle to the Venting position to quickly release the pressure. Press Cancel and remove the lid.

Use two forks to separate the spaghetti strands and mix the pasta and meat together. Taste the pasta. If it is a bit hard, return the cover to the pot and let warm for 5 minutes. Stir again and serve. Add more salt and pepper if needed.

ROUGHLY CHOPPED GARLIC

Place peeled cloves on your cutting board. Use a flat-blade or chef's knife with your hand on top to chop up and down, moving the pieces together if they spread, until you have pieces no bigger than ⅓ inch.

CHOLENT
WITH A TWIST

MEAT

HANDS-ON TIME:	11 Minutes if browning, 2 Minutes if not
TIME TO PRESSURE:	9 Minutes
COOKING TIME:	75 Minutes
RELEASE TYPE:	Quick Release
BUTTONS TO USE:	Sauté, if browning, and Pressure Cook
ADVANCE PREP:	May be made 2 days in advance

Serves 8–10

It seemed against the rules to make cholent in a pressure cooker, but I was truly amazed how thick and great it came out; the texture was perfect. My twist on the classic recipe is that I use sweet potatoes rather than white potatoes to lighten up the dish as I find cholent heavy enough. I also like the sweetness. You can use white potatoes if desired. Thanks to contributors to the Kosher Instant Pot® Facebook group who posted the barley, bean, and liquid amounts and cooking time. I make this two different ways. One method is to brown the meat and onions. The other way is to just throw everything in the pot. My tasters liked both, with a slight preference for the browned one. But know that if you do not want to take the time to brown the meat, the results will be delicious as well.

FOR THE SEARING METHOD:

Press Sauté and when the display reads "Hot," add the oil and meat to the inner pot in batches, for about 2 to 3 minutes per side. Remove browned pieces to a plate. Add the onions and cook for 2 minutes, stirring occasionally. Add the water and let bubble, and use a wooden spoon to scrape up the bottom of the pan. Press Cancel. Return the meat to the pot.

2 tablespoons oil

4 slices bone-in flanken, each cut in half

1 large onion, sliced

2 cups (473ml) water

2 cups (473ml) Beef Bone Broth (see page 49) or chicken stock or Vegetable Stock (see pages 44 and 47)

1 cup (200g) pearled barley

1 cup (200g) cholent bean mix, or your favorite beans

½ teaspoon turmeric

½ teaspoon cumin

½ teaspoon paprika

2 teaspoons garlic powder

½ teaspoon salt

½ teaspoon black pepper

1 pound (454g) sweet potatoes, peeled and cut into 3-inch (8cm) chunks

FOR THE EASY METHOD:

Place the oil, meat, onions, and water into the inner pot.

NEXT STEP FOR BOTH METHODS:

Add the stock, barley, beans, turmeric, cumin, paprika, garlic powder, salt, and pepper, and stir. Tuck in the sweet potato chunks.

Secure the lid, ensuring that the steam release handle is in the Sealing position. Press the Pressure Cook button and set the cooking time for 75 minutes. When the cooking time is complete, turn the steam release handle to the Venting position to quickly release the pressure. Press Cancel and remove the lid. Taste for seasonings. Add more salt and pepper as needed.

HOW TO KEEP WARM FOR SHABBAT

I know that the IP® has a slow cook setting but it did not make my cholent creamy enough, so I developed this method. I fully cook the cholent before Shabbat on the Pressure Cook setting. When the cooking time is complete, I quickly release the pressure. I then remove the electric lid and substitute a glass one sold on the IP® website. Then I press Slow Cook and set the time for after my lunch.

TEXAS CHILI

GLUTEN-FREE, MEAT

HANDS-ON TIME: 26 Minutes

TIME TO PRESSURE: 13 Minutes

COOKING TIME: 35 Minutes

BUTTONS TO USE: Sauté and Pressure Cook

RELEASE TYPE: Quick Release

ADVANCE PREP: May be made 2 days in advance or frozen

Serves 6–8

Many years ago, a friend made me chili from cut-up beef cubes, and it ruined me forever, as ground beef chili never tastes as good to me. This chili is just meat, spices, and a bit of tomato. I did not include beans, but there are versions of Texas chili with beans in them. The spice amount below has a bit of kick, but add more chile powder if you want really scorching chili (or less if you like a little less heat).

Press Sauté and when the display reads "Hot," add 1 tablespoon of the oil. Add the meat to the inner pot in 2 batches and cook each batch for 4 to 5 minutes, turning the meat pieces after 2 minutes. Stir occasionally until the meat is browned on all sides and remove to a bowl. Add another tablespoon of oil and repeat for the remaining meat.

Meanwhile, in a small bowl, combine the chile powder, cumin, coriander, cinnamon, oregano, cocoa, salt, and masa harina. Set aside.

When the last batch of meat is browned, transfer the meat and any liquid remaining in the pot into the bowl with the rest of the meat. Wipe the pot clean with a bunch of paper towels.

Add the remaining tablespoon of oil to the pot and add the onions and garlic. Cook for 4 to 5 minutes, stirring often, until they start to brown. Add ¼ cup (59ml) water and use a wooden spoon to scrape the bottom of the pot clean. Add the wine or beer and bring to a boil. Add the tomatoes, honey, spice mix, and another ½ cup (118ml) water and stir. Press Cancel and add the meat. Stir well.

CHILI

3 tablespoons oil, divided

2 to 2 ½ pounds (907g to 1kg) pepper steak, cut into 1-inch (2.5cm) pieces

2 teaspoons ancho or chipotle chile powder

1 tablespoon cumin

½ teaspoon ground coriander

¼ teaspoon cinnamon

½ teaspoon oregano

1 tablespoon unsweetened cocoa

1 teaspoon salt

1 tablespoon masa harina (ground cornmeal flour), or cornstarch

1 large onion, chopped into ½-inch (1.2cm) pieces, about 2 cups (473ml) chopped

ingredients continue on the following page

Secure the lid, ensuring that the steam release handle is in the Sealing position. Press the Pressure Cook button and set the cooking time for 35 minutes. When the cooking time is complete, turn the steam release handle to the Venting position to quickly release the pressure. Press Cancel and remove the lid.

Press Sauté and cook for 2 minutes to thicken, stirring occasionally.

Serve with non-dairy sour cream and cheese, rice, cubed avocado, green onions, and tortillas.

3 cloves garlic, finely chopped

¾ cup (177ml) water, divided

½ cup (118ml) wine or beer

½ cup (118ml) crushed tomatoes or tomato sauce

1 tablespoon honey

ESSENTIAL GARNISHES

non-dairy sour cream and cheese

rice (see page 146)

cubed avocado

sliced green onions

small corn tortillas

CHOPPING ONIONS

If you are chopping onions in a food processor, use the pulse feature until you have the desired size pieces. If you are chopping by hand, wear onion goggles (they really work!) or fill your mouth with water while you chop; this numbs your sinuses and prevents your eyes from tearing up.

SPINACH PESTO BRISKET

GLUTEN-FREE, MEAT,
PASSOVER

HANDS-ON TIME: 28 Minutes, best
made the day before
for neater slices

TIME TO PRESSURE: 9 Minutes

COOKING TIME: 70 Minutes

BUTTONS TO USE: Sauté and Pressure
Cook

RELEASE TYPE: Natural Release for
5 Minutes

ADVANCE PREP: May be made 2 days
in advance or frozen

The best part of my never-ending book tour is that I pick up new friends along the way. I met Edna Schrank when I was selling books at a conference and became closer the first of four times I was invited to speak at Congregation Beth Sholom of Northbrook, Illinois, a truly vibrant community in the Chicago suburbs. She is a leader in her shul and the Women's League of Conservative Judaism, a devoted mother and grandmother, and an obsessive cook and baker. She is also one of my best recipe testers. We came up with this idea together.

Serves 8

1 (4- to 5-pound [2kg to 2.2kg]) second-cut brisket, cut in half

3 cloves garlic, peeled

2 tablespoons almonds

24 large basil leaves, about 1-ounce (28g)

1 cup (30g) loosely packed spinach leaves

6 tablespoons (90ml) extra virgin olive oil

½ teaspoon salt

½ teaspoon black pepper, plus more to taste

2 tablespoons oil

2 large onions, halved and sliced

½ cup (118ml) water

kosher salt to taste

Press Sauté and make sure the device shows 30 minutes. When the display reads "Hot," add half of the meat to the inner pot and brown for about 3 to 4 minutes per side, until you see some crispy parts. Remove to a plate. Repeat for the other brisket half. Remove to the plate.

While the meat is browning, place the garlic and almonds into the bowl of the food processor and process until finely ground and they stick to the sides of the bowl. Scrape down the sides. Add the basil leaves and spinach and process until they are in very tiny pieces. Scrape down the bowl again and process for a few more seconds. Leave the machine on and pour the olive oil in slowly until it is all mixed in. Add the salt and pepper and pulse a few times.

When all of the meat has been browned and removed to a plate, add the oil and onions to the pot. Cook for 5 minutes, stirring occasionally, until the onions are browned. Add the water, let boil, and use a wooden spoon to scrape the bottom of the pot clean. Press Cancel.

Use a silicone spatula to spread 2 tablespoons of the pesto on top of each of the pieces of browned meat. If you have more than two pieces, divide the ¼ cup (59ml) of pesto among them. Return the meat to the pot, pesto side-up, pieces overlapping. Cover the remaining pesto with plastic and store in the fridge.

Secure the lid, ensuring that the steam release handle is in the Sealing position. Press the Pressure Cook button and set the cooking time for 70 minutes. When the cooking time is complete, let sit for 5 minutes to naturally release the pressure. Turn the steam release handle to the Venting position to release any remaining pressure. Press Cancel and remove the lid.

Remove the meat to a pan you can use to rewarm the brisket.

Press Sauté and when the mixture bubbles, add the reserved pesto, reserving 1½ tablespoons to add just before serving. Stir and cook for 4 minutes. Ladle some of the sauce on top of the meat so that at least half of the meat is submerged. Add some pepper on top and a generous pinch of kosher salt. Cover the meat and refrigerate until serving or it is cold enough to slice to freeze. Place the remaining sauce into a bowl, cover, and refrigerate until reheating.

Remove the fat from the meat and the sauce. Slice against the grain into ⅓-inch (8mm) slices, and if you are freezing the brisket, pour the remaining sauce and pesto on top and stir in. Cover tightly and freeze.

To serve the next day, cover the pan with foil and heat at 325°F (162°C) for 30 minutes, or until warm. Remove the foil, and add the remaining pesto by spooning some on top of the meat and stir some into the sauce. Reheat the remaining sauce and serve alongside.

> ### BRISKET CUTS
> *I prefer to cook with second-cut brisket as it has more fat and is therefore moister when cooked.*

PERSIAN LAMB AND HERB STEW

Every year on the Shabbat around Purim, I make a Persian dinner, as the story of Megilat Esther takes place in ancient Persia. You can use beef cubes instead of lamb if you like.

Press Sauté and when the display reads "Hot," add the oil and half of the lamb to the inner pot and stir to coat the meat with the oil. Cook for 5 minutes, turning occasionally, to brown all sides. Remove to a plate and repeat for the remaining lamb.

Add the onions, garlic, and green onions and cook for 3 minutes, stirring often. In a medium bowl, combine the mint, parsley, cilantro, and dill; scoop out 2 tablespoons and place into a small bowl and set aside. Add the remaining herbs, apple, saffron, and the saffron soaking water to the pot and stir, making sure nothing is stuck to the bottom of the pot. Add the lamb, salt, and pepper and stir.

Secure the lid, ensuring that the steam release handle is in the Sealing position. Press the Pressure Cook button and set the cooking time for 35 minutes. When the cooking time is complete, turn the steam release handle to the Venting position to quickly release the pressure. Remove the lid. Add the reserved herbs and lime zest and stir. Let device remain on Warm for 5 minutes and then serve.

GLUTEN-FREE, MEAT, PASSOVER

HANDS-ON TIME:	20 Minutes
TIME TO PRESSURE:	15 Minutes
COOKING TIME:	35 Minutes, plus 5 Minutes on Warm
BUTTONS TO USE:	Sauté and Pressure Cook
RELEASE TYPE:	Quick Release
ADVANCE PREP:	May be made 2 days in advance

Serves 6

2 tablespoons extra virgin olive oil

3 pounds (1.3kg) lamb cubes

2 onions, chopped into ½-inch (1.2cm) pieces

4 cloves garlic, chopped into small pieces

3 green onions, sliced

½ cup (12g) mint leaves, chopped

½ cup (12g) Italian parsley leaves, chopped

½ cup (12g) cilantro leaves, chopped

½ cup (5g) dill, chopped

1 yellow apple, cut into 1-inch (2.5cm) cubes

¼ teaspoon saffron threads dissolved in 1½ cups (354ml) hot water

¼ teaspoon salt

½ teaspoon black pepper

2 teaspoons lime zest, from 1 lime

MARRAKESH BEEF TAGINE WITH PRUNES AND PEANUTS

On our family trip to Morocco for vacation, we ate this tagine at the kosher restaurant in Marrakesh and then learned how to prepare it in a family cooking class. The addition of peanuts was a nice touch, but you can substitute other nuts or just omit them.

Press Sauté and when the display reads "Hot," add 2 tablespoons of the oil to the inner pot. Add the onions and cook for 10 to 15 minutes, stirring often, until the onions are browned. Do not let them burn. Remove to a bowl. While the onions cool, mix together the saffron, ginger, turmeric, cumin, salt, and pepper in a small bowl.

Add the remaining oil to the pot and brown the meat in two batches, turning often to brown all sides, for 6 to 7 minutes each batch, or until browned. Remove each batch to a plate. When all of the meat has been browned, add the hot water to the pot and cook, using a wooden spoon to scrape the bottom clean.

Add the spices, cinnamon sticks, and honey and stir. Add the meat and onions and stir.

Secure the lid, ensuring that the steam release handle is in the Sealing position. Press the Pressure Cook button and set the cooking time for 35 minutes. Turn the valve to the Venting

GLUTEN-FREE, MEAT, PASSOVER (WITHOUT PEANUTS)

HANDS-ON TIME:	30 Minutes
TIME TO PRESSURE:	12 Minutes for stew, plus 6 Minutes after adding prunes and peanuts
COOKING TIME:	35 Minutes for stew, plus 5 Minutes more for prunes and peanuts
BUTTONS TO USE:	Sauté and Pressure Cook
RELEASE TYPE:	Quick Release
ADVANCE PREP:	May be made 2 days in advance

Serves 8

3 tablespoons oil, divided

3 medium onions, halved and sliced

¼ teaspoon saffron threads

1 teaspoon ground ginger

1 teaspoon turmeric

1 teaspoon cumin

1 teaspoon salt

1 teaspoon black pepper

2½–3 pounds (1–1.3kg) beef cubes

1½ cups (354ml) hot water

2 cinnamon sticks

2 tablespoons honey

1 cup (174g) pitted prunes

⅓ cup (51g) unsalted, dry roasted peanuts

position to quickly release the pressure. Press Cancel and remove the lid.

Add the prunes and peanuts. Secure the lid, ensuring that the steam release handle is in the Sealing position. Press the Pressure Cook button and set the cooking time for 5 minutes. Turn the valve to the Venting position to quickly release the pressure. Press Cancel and remove the lid.

SPICY RIBS WITH COFFEE AND CHILI SAUCE

GLUTEN-FREE, MEAT, PASSOVER

HANDS-ON TIME:	10 Minutes to soak chilies, 28 Minutes prep
TIME TO PRESSURE:	17 Minutes
COOKING TIME:	40 Minutes
BUTTONS TO USE:	Sauté and Pressure Cook
RELEASE TYPE:	Quick Release
ADVANCE PREP:	May be made 2 days in advance or frozen

Serves 6–8

The first food I ever cooked in my IP® was short ribs/flanken, and it is what convinced me that this device would change my life. I was amazed how moist the meat was after 40 minutes, when it usually took 2½ hours of baking time to achieve the same melt-in-your-mouth texture.

Place the chiles and ½ cup of the hot water into a small bowl and let sit for 10 minutes. Press Sauté and when the display reads "Hot," add the oil and ribs to the inner pot 3 or 4 pieces at a time, and sear for 3 minutes per side. Remove to a plate. Repeat for the remaining meat. Add the remaining hot water and use a wooden spoon to scrape the bottom of the pot clean. Press Cancel.

When the meat is almost done browning, place the chiles and soaking water, onion, garlic, maple syrup, lime juice, brewed and ground coffee, chili powder, Aleppo pepper, and salt into a food processor or blender and process until smooth, for about 1 minute.

When all of the meat has been browned, add the sauce to the pan, return the meat to the pan, and turn to coat each piece.

Secure the lid, ensuring that the steam release handle is in the Sealing position. Press the Pressure Cook button and set the cooking time for 40 minutes. When the cooking time is complete, turn the valve to the Venting position to quickly release the pressure. Press Cancel and remove the lid.

Remove the meat to a serving dish. Press Sauté and cook the liquid for 5 minutes to reduce. Pour over the meat.

2 large dried red chiles

1 cup (236ml) hot water, divided

1 tablespoon oil

4½–6 pounds (2–2.7kg) flanken, cut in half

1 medium onion, quartered

3 cloves garlic

3 tablespoons maple syrup

2 tablespoons fresh lime juice, from 1–2 limes

½ cup (118ml) brewed coffee

2 tablespoons ground or instant coffee

1¼ teaspoons chili powder

¼ teaspoon Aleppo pepper or red pepper flakes

1 teaspoon salt

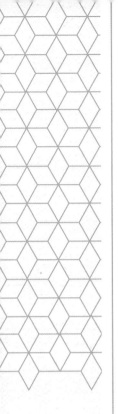

VEGETARIAN MAINS

RIGATONI IN PINK SAUCE

My son Jake is a terrific cook, and pasta in pink sauce has been one of his favorites to prepare since he was old enough to reach the stovetop. I tried cooking the pasta and sauce together in the Instant Pot®, but it never cooked as well as it did when done in separate steps. Feel free to add more red chile flakes for more kick.

Press Sauté and when the display reads "Hot," add the oil, onions, and garlic to the inner pot. Cook for 3 minutes, stirring often. Press Cancel. Add the water, red pepper flakes, and salt and stir. Add the pasta and stir.

Secure the lid, ensuring that the steam release handle is in the Sealing position. Press the Pressure Cook button and set the cooking time for 7 minutes. When the cooking time is complete, turn the steam release handle to the Venting position to quickly release the pressure. Remove the lid and let the pot remain on Warm. Stir the pasta. Add the tomato sauce, half and half or cream, and pepper, stir, and let warm for 5 minutes. Press Cancel. Stir again and serve with the basil sprinkled on top. Add Parmesan cheese if desired.

DAIRY

HANDS-ON TIME:	8 Minutes
TIME TO PRESSURE:	9–10 Minutes
COOKING TIME:	7 Minutes, plus 5 minutes on Warm
BUTTON TO USE:	Pressure Cook
RELEASE TYPE:	Quick Release
ADVANCE PREP:	May be made 1 day in advance

Serves 6

2 tablespoons extra virgin olive oil

½ medium onion chopped into ¼-inch (6mm) pieces, heaping ½ cup (118ml) chopped

3 cloves garlic, finely chopped

4 cups (1 liter) water

2 pinches red pepper flakes

½ teaspoon salt

1 pound (454g) rigatoni

2 cups (473ml) tomato sauce

½ cup (118ml) half and half or heavy cream

¼ teaspoon black pepper

3 large basil leaves, chiffonade, see below

grated Parmesan cheese, if desired

BASIL CHIFFONADE

Stack basil leaves and then roll them up the long way. Cut across the rolls to create very thin slices.

NORMA'S MACARONI AND CHEESE

Norma Amado was our nanny when my twins were born. I remember fondly how she brought five-year-old Emily and three-year-old Sam to visit me when I was on bed rest in the hospital for three weeks before Jake and Joey were born. She made and brought me lunch on every visit. Norma is Peruvian and gave us our first taste of Peruvian food, yet this classic American macaroni and cheese has nourished us for twenty years. It was years before my kids discovered that other people eat mac and cheese from a box and asked me why our version wasn't orange.

Place the pasta and water into the inner pot and stir. Secure the lid, ensuring that the steam release handle is in the Sealing position. Press the Pressure Cook button and set the cooking time for 6 minutes. When the cooking time is complete, turn the steam release handle to Venting to quickly release the pressure.

Use a wooden spoon to break apart the macaroni, scraping up the bottom of the pot and mixing the remaining water into the pasta. Press Cancel.

Press Sauté. Add the salt and some pepper and mix in. Add the milk, butter, and cheese and cook, stirring the entire time, until the cheese has melted and the mixture is creamy, for about 4 minutes. Taste and add more salt and pepper as needed. Add Parmesan cheese if desired.

If reheating the next day, add a bit more milk and mix in before reheating.

DAIRY

HANDS-ON TIME: 5 Minutes

TIME TO PRESSURE: 12 Minutes

COOKING TIME: 6 Minutes

BUTTONS TO USE: Sauté and Pressure Cook

RELEASE TYPE: Quick Release

ADVANCE PREP: May be made 1 day in advance

Serves: 4–6

1 pound (454g) elbow pasta

4 cups (1 liter) water

¾ teaspoon salt, or more as needed

black pepper to taste

½ cup (118ml) whole milk

2 tablespoons (28g) butter

3 cups (336g) shredded cheddar cheese

grated Parmesan cheese, optional

TOFU TIKKA MASALA

Indian food always demands a lot of chopping time, and even though this recipe has some steps with waiting time, you can go do something else while components of the dish sit. The actual cooking time is super short. While the tofu is draining, prepare the marinade for it, start the curry sauce, and then cut the tofu. Serve with rice (see page 146).

Place a large colander into the sink. Line with 2 layers of paper towel, add the tofu, more paper towel on top, and place something heavy, such as a small saucepan, on top. Let the tofu drain for 20 minutes.

Meanwhile, prepare the marinade for the tofu. Place the yogurt, coriander, turmeric, garam masala, chile powder, paprika, and salt into a large bowl and whisk well. Set aside.

While waiting for the tofu to drain, make the curry sauce. Press Sauté and when device reads "Hot," add the coconut oil to the inner pot. Add the cinnamon stick and cumin seeds and let sit for about 1 to 2 minutes, until the cumin seeds start to pop. Add the onions, red pepper, garlic, ginger, and jalapeño and cook for 4 minutes, stirring occasionally.

Add the tomatoes, tomato paste, curry powder, red chili powder, sugar, water, 2 tablespoons of the cilantro, and salt. Mix well and cook for 2 minutes, scraping the bottom well with a wooden spoon. Press Cancel. Secure the lid, ensuring

PARVE, VEGAN

HANDS-ON TIME: 20 Minutes to drain the tofu, 15 Minutes to marinate tofu, prep time 12 Minutes

TIME TO PRESSURE: 8 Minutes

COOKING TIME: 2 Minutes

BUTTONS TO USE: Sauté and Pressure Cook

RELEASE TYPE: Quick Release

ADVANCE PREP: May be made 2 days in advance

Serves 8

TOFU AND MARINADE

21 ounces (595g) firm tofu, water drained

1 (5.3-ounce [157ml]) container dairy-free coconut yogurt

2 teaspoons ground coriander

1 teaspoon turmeric

2 teaspoons garam masala

½ teaspoon red chili powder

1 teaspoon smoked paprika

½ teaspoon salt

CURRY SAUCE

1 tablespoon coconut oil

1 cinnamon stick

½ teaspoon cumin seeds

ingredients continue on the following page

that the steam release handle is in the Sealing position. Press the Pressure Cook button and set the cooking time for 2 minutes.

Turn the steam release handle to the Venting position to quickly release the pressure. Press Cancel. Remove the cinnamon stick. Add the coconut cream and lemon juice and use an immersion blender to purée the curry.

After the tofu has drained, place onto a cutting board the way it was in the container, with the longer side facing you. Slice vertically into 5 strips, about ½- to ¾-inch (1.2- to 2cm) thick, and then turn each strip flat and cut in half vertically. Slice into 1- to 1½-inch (about 6 to 10cm) cubes. Add the tofu cubes to the marinade and stir to coat. Let marinate for 15 minutes.

To the curry, add the tofu with the yogurt marinade and the chickpeas and mix gently. Press Sauté and after about 3 minutes, when the mixture comes to a boil, cook for another 3 minutes, stirring often and gently, without breaking up the tofu. Taste the sauce for salt and pepper and add more as needed. Place into a serving bowl and sprinkle the remaining cilantro on top.

1 large red onion, cut into ½-inch (1.2cm) pieces

1 red pepper, cut into ½-inch (1.2cm) pieces

5 cloves garlic, roughly chopped

1 piece (1½ inches [1.2cm]) of ginger, cut into small pieces

1 jalapeño, seeded and chopped

2 large tomatoes, seeded and cut into 2-inch (5cm) pieces

3 tablespoons tomato paste

2 teaspoons curry powder

¼ teaspoon red chili powder

1 tablespoon sugar

¾ cup (177ml) water

3 tablespoons chopped cilantro, divided

1 teaspoon salt

black pepper, to taste

½ cup (118ml) coconut cream, the thick kind

2 tablespoons fresh lemon juice

1 cup (152g) canned chickpeas, drained

COCONUT OIL

I use coconut oil in many recipes, both savory and sweet, and I always use it in Indian food. If you do not like the coconut taste or are allergic, you can substitute another type of oil.

ASIAN NOODLES

This is the type of dish that I have on deck whenever my children are home because they often want food to snack on other than my baked goods. They will eat this for "second dinner" at 9:00 pm and for their midnight snack.

PARVE, VEGETARIAN

HANDS-ON TIME: 4 Minutes

TIME TO PRESSURE: 11 Minutes

COOKING TIME: 6 Minutes

BUTTON TO USE: Pressure Cook

RELEASE TYPE: Quick Release

ADVANCE PREP: May be made 2 days in advance

Serves 6–8

Place the water into the inner pot. Grab handfuls of linguine, rinse under water, and then break in half. Add to the pot, separating the strands as much as possible and placing them in different directions. Drizzle the oil on top and use tongs or your hands to turn and coat the strands with the oil. Press as much pasta as you can into the water.

Secure the lid, ensuring that the steam release handle is in the Sealing position. Press the Pressure Cook button and set the time for 6 minutes.

While the pasta is cooking, dissolve the peanut butter into the boiling water with a whisk. Add the soy sauce, mirin, sesame oil, ginger, honey, sugar, and red pepper flakes and whisk well.

When the cooking time is complete, turn the steam release handle to the Venting position to quickly release the pressure. Remove the lid. Press Cancel.

Use a fork to break apart the pasta strands and stir. Pour the sauce into the pasta and mix well. Transfer to a large serving bowl and sprinkle the green onions and the sesame seeds on top. Serve warm or cold.

3 cups (710ml) water

1 pound (454g) linguine

1 tablespoon oil

½ cup (128g) peanut butter, preferably the natural kind, mixed well before measuring

1 cup (236ml) boiling water

½ cup (118ml) soy sauce

1 tablespoon mirin

2 tablespoons toasted sesame oil

¼ teaspoon ground ginger

1 tablespoon honey

1 tablespoon sugar

¼ teaspoon red pepper flakes

3 green onions, sliced

1 tablespoon toasted sesame seeds

RED LENTIL DAL AND RICE

This recipe provides a complete meal in one cooking step and it has protein, fiber, potassium, folate, and manganese. It is also really delicious.

Press Sauté and when the display reads "Hot," add the coconut oil to the inner pot. Add the onions, garlic, ginger, and jalapeño and cook for 3 minutes, stirring occasionally. Add the tomatoes, cumin, coriander, and turmeric and cook for 2 minutes, stirring often. Press Cancel. Rinse the lentils and dump them into the pot. Break up the wet lentils if they stick together. Add the water, red pepper flakes, salt, black pepper, and cilantro and stir.

Place the steam rack on top of the dal. Place the rice, water, and salt into a 6- or 7-inch (15cm or 18cm) round pan and stir. Wrap the bottom of the pan with aluminum foil so that the turmeric does not stain your pan. Create an aluminum foil sling (see page xi). Place the pan on the foil and lift up the sides to insert the pan on top of the steam rack.

Secure the lid, ensuring that the steam release handle is in the Sealing position. Press the Pressure Cook button and set the cooking time for 6 minutes. When the cooking time is complete, let sit for 10 minutes to naturally release the pressure. Turn the steam release handle to the Venting position to release any remaining pressure.

PARVE, VEGAN

HANDS-ON TIME: 24 Minutes

COOKING TIME: 6 Minutes

TIME TO PRESSURE: 13 Minutes

BUTTONS TO USE: Sauté and Pressure Cook

RELEASE TYPE: Natural Release for 10 Minutes

ADVANCE PREP: May be made 2 days in advance

Serves 6

DAL

2 tablespoons coconut or other oil

2 medium onions, finely chopped

4 cloves garlic, finely chopped

1 tablespoon finely chopped ginger

1 jalapeño, seeded, finely chopped

2 medium tomatoes, cut into small dice

1 teaspoon cumin

1 teaspoon ground coriander

1 teaspoon turmeric

1 cup (198g) red lentils

3 cups (710ml) water

¾ teaspoon red pepper flakes, or more for more kick

1 teaspoon salt

½ teaspoon black pepper

1 cup (25g) cilantro leaves, chopped, plus more for garnish

ingredients continue on the following page

Remove the lid and use the sides of the sling to lift the rice pan off the rack onto a plate (the bottom is dirty). Stir the dal. Add more salt and pepper as needed, and more cilantro if desired. Fluff the rice with a fork.

1½ cups (228g) basmati rice, rinsed

1½ cups (354ml) water

¼ teaspoon salt

BLACK BEAN CHILI

PARVE, VEGAN

HANDS-ON TIME: 5 Minutes

COOKING TIME: 2 Minutes

TIME TO PRESSURE: 10 Minutes

BUTTONS TO USE: Sauté and Pressure

RELEASE TYPE: Quick Release

ADVANCE PREP: May be made 3 days
in advance

Serves 6

This is a version of a staple in the Shoyer household. It is a "survival recipe," one you need to teach your kids before they leave home. They can vary it with different types of beans and add other vegetables they have on hand, all cut into ½-inch (1.2cm) pieces. Every summer I teach this recipe to campers at Camp Ramah New England, and on the last day of the course, we clean out the fridge with this dish: some favorite additions are sweet potato, carrot, and zucchini cubes, and any chopped herbs.

Press Sauté and when the display reads "Hot," add the oil and onions to the inner pot. Cook for 2 minutes, stirring occasionally. Add the garlic, pepper, tomato, and jalapeño and cook for another 2 minutes. Add the cumin, paprika, salt, pepper, water, beans, and half of the cilantro. Stir.

Secure the lid, ensuring that the steam release handle is in the Sealing position. Press the Pressure Cook button and set the cooking time for 2 minutes. When the cooking time is complete, turn the steam release handle to the Venting position to quickly release the pressure. Remove the lid. Add the remaining cilantro, lime zest, and more salt and pepper as needed. Serve with the green onions on top.

2 tablespoons oil

1 small onion, chopped into ¼-inch (6mm) pieces

3 cloves garlic, minced

1 yellow or red pepper, cut into ⅓-inch (8mm) pieces

1 medium tomato, seeded and chopped

½ jalapeño, seeded and chopped fine, optional

1 teaspoon cumin

½ teaspoon paprika

¼ teaspoon salt

¼ teaspoon black pepper

½ cup (118ml) water

2 (15-ounce cans [444ml]) black beans, drained and rinsed with water

½ cup (12g) cilantro leaves, chopped, divided

1 teaspoon lime zest, from 1 lime

2 green onions, sliced

TRIMMING GREEN ONIONS

Cut off the very end of the white part and of the dark green end. Peel down the outer green layer toward the white part and discard. Rinse well.

WILD MUSHROOM RISOTTO

Risotto is one of those dishes that requires a lot of attention, adding the stock a little at a time and cooking it down before adding more. The IP® creates creamy risotto with little effort. It is best prepared right before eating for the creamiest risotto.

Press Sauté and when the display reads "Hot," add the oil, onions, shallots, garlic, and both types of mushrooms to the inner pot, and cook for 5 minutes, stirring occasionally, to soften. Add the wine and cook for 3 minutes, stirring often. Add the rice, salt, and pepper and stir. Cook for 1 minute, stirring the whole time. Add the stock and stir well, making sure nothing is stuck to the bottom of the pot. Press Cancel.

Secure the lid, ensuring that the steam release handle is in the Sealing position. Press the Pressure Cook button and set the cooking time for 6 minutes.

When the cooking time is complete, turn the steam release handle to the Venting position to quickly release the pressure. Press Cancel and remove the lid.

Add the cheese, stir, and return the cover to the pot, then press Warm. Let sit for 8 minutes. Stir again. Add a little more salt and pepper. If desired, drizzle the truffle oil.

CLEANING MUSHROOMS

Rinse them under the faucet with a light stream of water and use your fingers to wipe off any dirt. Use paper towel to dry the mushrooms and wipe off any remaining dirt.

DAIRY, GLUTEN-FREE

HANDS-ON TIME:	20 Minutes
TIME TO PRESSURE:	7 Minutes
COOKING TIME:	6 Minutes, let warm for 8 Minutes after you add the cheese
BUTTONS TO USE:	Sauté and Pressure Cook
RELEASE TYPE:	Quick Release
ADVANCE PREP:	May be made 1 day in advance

Serves 6

3 tablespoons extra virgin olive oil

1 small onion, chopped into ¼-inch (6mm) pieces

1 shallot, thinly sliced

2 cloves garlic, finely chopped

8 ounces (227g) white mushrooms, chopped into ½-inch (1.2cm) pieces

10 shiitake mushrooms, sliced

⅓ cup (79ml) white wine

1 cup (200g) Arborio rice

½ teaspoon salt

¼ teaspoon black pepper

2½ cups (591ml) hot Vegetable Stock (see page 44)

⅓ cup (28g) grated Parmesan cheese

truffle oil to garnish, optional

WHITE BEAN AND LEEK STEW

This has been one of my go-to recipes dishes when I find out at the last minute that a vegetarian or vegan is coming to dinner. You should always have a few cans of beans in your pantry to throw together a vegetarian or vegan main course as needed.

Press Sauté and when the display reads "Hot," add the oil, leeks, onions, and shallots to the inner pot and cook for 3 minutes. Add the garlic, rosemary, bay leaf, and thyme and cook for 1 minute. Add the stock and use a wooden spoon to scrape the bottom of the pot clean. Add the beans, salt, and pepper and stir.

Secure the lid, ensuring that the steam release handle is in the Sealing position. Press the Pressure Cook button and set the cooking time for 1 minute.

Meanwhile, prepare the parsley pesto. Place the garlic and almonds into the bowl of the food processor and process unti they are finely ground and stick to the sides of the bowl. Scrape down the sides. Add the parsley and process until it is in very tiny pieces. Scrape down the bowl again and process for a few more seconds. Add the salt. Leave the machine on and pour the olive oil in slowly until it is all mixed in.

When the cooking time is complete, turn the steam release handle to the Venting position to quickly release the pressure. Remove the lid.

GLUTEN-FREE, PARVE, VEGAN

HANDS-ON TIME:	7 Minutes
TIME TO PRESSURE:	20 Minutes
COOKING TIME:	1 Minute
BUTTONS TO USE:	Sauté and Pressure
RELEASE TYPE:	Quick Release
ADVANCE PREP:	May be made 2 days in advance

Serves 6

STEW

2 tablespoons extra virgin olive oil

2 leeks, white and light green only, sliced into ¾-inch (2cm) pieces

1 small onion, chopped

1 shallot, chopped into ½-inch (1.2cm) pieces

3 cloves garlic, roughly chopped

½ teaspoon finely chopped rosemary leaves

1 bay leaf

2 sprigs fresh thyme

1 cup (236ml) Vegetable Stock (see page 44)

2 (15-ounce [444ml]) cans cannellini beans, drained and rinsed

¼ teaspoon salt

¼ teaspoon black pepper

ingredients continue on the following page

Remove the thyme stems and bay leaf. Add the collard greens and 1 tablespoon of the pesto. Secure the lid and let sit on Warm for 5 minutes. Press Cancel. If serving immediately, stir in the remaining pesto and serve. If reheating later, only mix in 2 tablespoons of the pesto and reserve the rest to add in after reheating.

2 cups (112g) chopped collard greens, about 1½-inch (4cm) pieces (or 2 handfuls from a bag of pre-washed collards)

PARSLEY PESTO

1 clove garlic

2 tablespoons whole almonds, with or without skin

¾ cup (18g) loosely packed Italian parsley leaves

¼ teaspoon salt

3 tablespoons extra virgin olive oil

ADDITIONS

If you have 1– 1½ cups of leftover chicken, turkey, or beef, add it to the pot when you add the collard greens and press Sauté. Cook until heated through.

VEGAN ZUCCHINI ROLLS WITH CASHEW CHEESE

In 2018, Keren Brown, Israeli food writer and expert on all things food in Tel Aviv, took me on a tour of vegan restaurants in Tel Aviv, the vegan capital of the world. During our tour, we ate these wonderful rolls made with vegan cheese. I make the cheese with cashews, and the texture is like ricotta. I use jarred tomato sauce in this recipe, but you can also use 1½ cups (354ml) of your own homemade sauce. This is a great main dish for a vegan guest or even a cute appetizer on a small plate. You can always make these dairy by spreading them with ricotta cheese mixed with the lemon juice, finely chopped basil, salt, and pepper.

About 20 minutes prior to processing the cheese, slice the zucchinis vertically (the long way) into ¼-inch (6mm) pieces. You can use the mandoline if you are very brave, but as I have injured myself too many times using it, I use a knife to cut the slices by turning the zucchini on its side and then carefully cutting the long slices. You can also use a sharp paring knife to thin out the slices after they are cut. Any rejects or end pieces can be saved in the fridge or freezer for soup or the vegetable stock on page 44. You will need 8 slices for this dish, but I always slice 9 or 10 pieces so I can use the most pliable ones for the recipe, reserving the rejects for soup.

Line a cookie sheet with two layers of paper towels. Place the zucchini slices on top. Sprinkle the salt over the slices and let

GLUTEN-FREE, PARVE, VEGAN, PASSOVER

ADVANCE PREP:	Soak cashews for 5 hours, soften zucchini for at least 15 minutes and as long as 1 hour
HANDS-ON TIME:	12 Minutes
TIME TO PRESSURE:	10 Minutes
COOKING TIME:	6 Minutes
BUTTON TO USE:	Pressure Cook
RELEASE TYPE:	Quick Release
ADVANCE PREP:	Cashew Cheese or completed dish may be made 2 days in advance

Serves 4–6 as a side dish or 2–3 as a main course.

CASHEW CHEESE

1 cup (138g) raw cashews, soaked in 1 cup (236ml) of cold water for 5 hours

2 teaspoons lemon juice, from 1 lemon

¼ cup (59ml) water

4 large basil leaves

½ teaspoon salt

pinch black pepper

ingredients continue on the following page

them sit for 15 minutes. Rinse the slices with cold water and dry them. Line the cookie sheet with a fresh layer of paper towels and place the zucchini slices on top to dry further.

To make the cheese, drain the cashews and place them into a food processor. Add the lemon juice, water, basil, salt, and pepper and process into a paste, scraping down the sides of the bowl multiple times.

Place the steam rack into the inner pot and add 1 cup of water. You will need a 6- or 7-inch (15cm or 18cm) pan to make this recipe; I prefer the 7-inch (18cm) one. Add the marinara sauce to the pan.

To make the rolls, take one of the zucchini slices and spread about 1½ tablespoons of the cheese over the entire slice to the edges. Roll up from the smaller end. One side of the roll may be prettier so that part should face up. Place the roll into the sauce, leaning the end of the roll into the side of the pan to keep it from unrolling. Repeat for the other rolls and place one or two into the center.

Create an aluminum foil sling (see page xi). Place the pan on the foil and lift up the sides to insert the pan on top of the steam rack.

Secure the lid, ensuring that the steam release handle is in the Sealing position. Press the Pressure Cook button and set the cooking time for 6 minutes. When the cooking time is complete, press Cancel and turn the steam release handle to the Venting position to quickly release the pressure. To serve, scoop up a roll and place it on a plate, adding more sauce around it.

ZUCCHINI ROLLS

2 large zucchinis, about 1 pound, 3 ounces (590g) total

1½ teaspoons salt

1½ cups (354ml) marinara sauce

POACHED SALMON WITH MUSTARD DILL SAUCE

The Instant Pot® creates the moistest salmon I have ever eaten in my life. The only challenge is that you can only poach 1 pound at a time. You can always make more in batches, since second and later batches come to pressure faster once the device is hot. You can poach more salmon as needed, as the sauce is enough for 3–4 pounds of salmon.

Place the water into the inner pot. Add the steam rack and place the dill on the rack and the lemon slices on top of the dill. Place the salmon on top.

Secure the lid, ensuring that the steam release handle is in the Sealing position. Press the Steam button and set the cooking time for 4 minutes.

Meanwhile, prepare the sauce. Place the mustard, sugar, dry mustard, and vinegar into the bowl of a food processor. With the machine running, slowly pour in the oil and process until the mixture is thick. Add the dill and process for another minute.

When the cooking time is complete, press Cancel and turn the steam release handle to the Venting position to quickly release the pressure. Carefully lift the steam rack and fish to remove. Add salt and pepper to taste. Serve with the sauce.

GLUTEN-FREE, PARVE

HANDS-ON TIME: 4 Minutes
TIME TO PRESSURE: 9 Minutes
STEAM TIME: 4 Minutes
BUTTON TO USE: Steam
RELEASE TYPE: Quick Release
ADVANCE PREP: May be made 2 days in advance

Serves 2

SALMON

1 cup (236ml) water

1 cup (25g) dill, include stems

5–6 slices lemon, from 1 lemon

1 pound (454g) salmon filet

salt and black pepper to taste

SAUCE

½ cup (118ml) Dijon mustard

4 tablespoons sugar

2 teaspoons dry mustard

4 tablespoons (59ml) white vinegar

⅔ cup (158ml) canola oil

1 cup (10g) dill leaves

ASIAN SALMON

PARVE

HANDS-ON TIME:	6 Minutes
TIME TO PRESSURE:	6 Minutes
COOKING TIME:	2 Minutes for pink, 3 Minutes more medium-well
BUTTONS TO USE:	Sauté and Pressure Cook
RELEASE TYPE:	Quick Release
ADVANCE PREP:	May be made 2 days in advance

One batch serves 2

The sauce for this recipe is sufficient to cook a family's worth of salmon, but you have to cook the fish in batches. It does, however, cook quickly. Remove the first filet and then repeat the process without cooking down the sauce. Repeat as needed. Each 1-pound (454g) filet serves two people.

1 tablespoon oil

3 tablespoons soy sauce

1 tablespoon chopped fresh ginger

2 tablespoons honey

2 teaspoons orange zest

⅔ cup (158ml) fresh orange juice, from 1–2 oranges

1 tablespoon mirin

2 teaspoons toasted sesame oil

1 pound (454g) salmon filet

2 green onions, thinly sliced

Place the oil, soy sauce, ginger, honey, orange zest and juice, mirin, and sesame oil into a small bowl and whisk well. Press Sauté and when the display reads "Hot," add the sauce to the inner pot. Once the mixture bubbles, after about 30 seconds, add the salmon topside down. Let the salmon brown for 1 minute.

Press Cancel. Secure the lid, ensuring that the steam release handle is in the Sealing position. Press the Pressure Cook button and set the cooking time for 2 minutes.

When the cooking time is complete, press Cancel and turn the steam release handle to the Venting position to quickly release the pressure. Carefully remove the salmon to a plate. If you are making more salmon, press Sauté, add the second piece, let brown for 2 minutes, and then pressure cook as you did the first piece. When you are done cooking the salmon, press Sauté and cook the sauce for 2 to 3 minutes, or until reduced and thickened a bit.

Pour the sauce over the fish, sprinkle the green onions on top, and serve. If desired, broil the fish for 1 minute to brown a bit more.

THAI RED CURRY FISH

Over the past ten years, more and more Asian products are being certified kosher. I had tried to find kosher red curry paste and was told it was only available in Israel. Ask friends to bring it back for you, as it lasts a while once opened. This recipe includes how to make the paste yourself if you cannot find it ready made.

To make the red curry paste, grind the cumin, coriander, and peppercorns together in a spice or coffee grinder. Place into the food processor. Add the chiles and the soaking water, ginger, lemongrass, lime zest and juice, shallot, fish sauce, garlic, tomato paste, and chili powder. Process until you have a paste. You will need to stop and scrape down the sides a few times.

To make the fish, press Sauté and when the device reads "Hot," add the oil to the inner pot. Add the onions, shallots, garlic, ginger, and jalapeño and cook for 4 minutes, stirring occasionally. Press Cancel. Add the coconut milk and then fill the can halfway with water and add to the pot. Add the fish sauce, ¼ cup of the red curry paste, chili powder, salt, and half of the basil leaves and stir.

Place the fish pieces into the sauce, the thicker ones on the bottom, and use a large spoon to scoop up some sauce to cover the top of the fish. Secure the lid, ensuring that the steam release handle is in the Sealing position. Press the Pressure Cook button and set the cooking time for 2 minutes. When the cooking time is complete, turn the steam release handle to the Venting position to quickly release the pressure.

GLUTEN-FREE, PARVE

HANDS-ON TIME:	30 Minutes if making the paste, 20 Minutes prep
TIME TO PRESSURE:	12 Minutes
COOKING TIME:	2 Minutes
BUTTONS TO USE:	Sauté and Pressure Cook
RELEASE TYPE:	Quick Release
ADVANCE PREP:	May be made 1 day in advance, paste can be made 2 months in advance

Serves 6

RED CURRY PASTE

1 teaspoon cumin seeds

2 teaspoons coriander seeds

½ teaspoon black peppercorns

¼ cup small 2-inch (5cm) dried red chiles (about 2 whole), soaked in ¼ cup (59ml) water for 25 minutes

1-inch (2.5cm) chunk fresh ginger

1 teaspoon lemongrass, chopped, or paste

½ teaspoon lime zest plus juice of half lime

1 shallot, halved

2 tablespoons fish sauce

3 cloves garlic

2 tablespoons tomato paste

1 teaspoon chili powder

ingredients continue on the following page

Lift up the fish pieces and place them into a deep serving dish. Cover to keep warm. Add the remaining basil, cilantro, lime zest, and hot sauce to taste to the sauce and stir. Let sit for 1 minute. Pour the sauce on top of the fish and serve.

FISH

2 tablespoons oil

1 red onion, chopped into ¼-inch (6mm) pieces

1 shallot, halved and sliced

4 cloves garlic, roughly chopped

1 tablespoon finely chopped ginger, about a 2-inch (5cm) piece

1 jalapeño, seeded and finely chopped

1 can coconut milk (the creamy kind)

2 tablespoons fish sauce

¼ cup (57g) red curry paste

1 teaspoon chili powder

½ teaspoon salt

4 large basil leaves, chiffonade (see page 124), divided

2 pounds (907g) cod loin, cut into 6 pieces

½ cup (12g) cilantro leaves, chopped

2 teaspoons lime zest, from 1 lime

1 teaspoon Sriracha, or other hot sauce, or more to taste

SIDE DISHES

RICE 101

For All the Methods:

- Rinse the rice first in a colander

- Use a 1:1 ratio of rice to water

- Add ¼ teaspoon salt

- Full natural release (takes no more than 18 minutes)

You can also add other dry spices, chopped fresh herbs, citrus juice, soy sauce, or other flavoring to the water and rice. Another variation is to cook the rice in Vegetable Stock (see page 44), chicken stock (see page 47), or Beef Bone Broth (see page 49).

Rice Setting

The IP® has a "Rice" button that can be used for regular white rice. Add the same amount of water as rice and place into the inner pot. Do not add an amount of rice or water that goes over the fill line inside the pot. Press the Rice button and allow the rice to cook. Do a full natural release, allowing the pot to sit until the pin drops and you can open the lid. Remove the lid, fluff the rice, and serve.

If you are preparing other types of rice, then use the manual program as explained below.

Manual Cooking

To cook rice manually, place the rice and water into the inner pot. Secure the lid, ensuring that the steam release handle is in the Sealing position. Press the Pressure Cook button and set the cooking time according to the chart below. When the cooking time is complete, let the pot sit until all of the pressure has been released naturally and the pin drops. Open the lid and fluff the rice.

- **Basmati and Jasmine:** 6 minutes

- **Brown rice:** 24 minutes

- **Sushi rice:** 2 minutes—some suggest soaking the rice in water for 20 minutes before draining well and cooking

- **Wild rice:** 25 minutes

Pot-in-Pot Cooking

Place the rice and water as indicated in the recipe (not more than will fit with a little room at the top) into a 6- to 7-inch (15cm to 18cm) round pan. Add 1 cup of water and some salt to the inner pot. Insert the steam rack. Create an aluminum sling (see page xi). Place the pan on top of the sling and lift the side to insert the pan into the pot on top of the steam rack. Press the Pressure Cook button and set the cooking time for 6 minutes for white rice, 22 for brown and wild rice.

The first time I used this method to cook my main course and rice at the same time I was amazed at the simplicity. The steam rack that comes with your IP® fits over a stew made of small pieces, like legumes or chopped meat. You can also buy a steam rack with taller legs to fit above bigger quantities or larger pieces of food. Place the rack on top of the stew, then insert the steam rack and pan of rice and water on top. I use this method for the Red Lentil Dal and Rice (see page 130).

LENTILS AND RICE WITH SPICED ONIONS

GLUTEN-FREE, PARVE, VEGAN

HANDS-ON TIME:	18 Minutes
TIME TO PRESSURE:	9 Minutes
COOKING TIME:	15 Minutes
BUTTON TO USE:	Pressure Cook
RELEASE TYPE:	Natural Release for 10 Minutes
ADVANCE PREP:	May be made 2 days in advance

Serves 6–8

There are two steps to this recipe because it tasted so much better that way. When this dish is first cooked, the texture is a bit too wet for my taste, so I let it sit for an hour or so to dry it out before serving. It is even better the next day.

Place the rice, lentils, water, and salt into the inner pot. Secure the lid, ensuring that the steam release handle is in the Sealing position. Press the Pressure Cook button and set the cooking time for 15 minutes.

Meanwhile, in a large frying pan, heat 2 tablespoons of the oil over medium-high heat. Add the onions and cook for 10 to 15 minutes, stirring often, to brown the onions completely. If they start to burn, reduce the heat. Reduce heat to medium-low and add the remaining oil. Add the garlic, turmeric, cumin, paprika, Aleppo or chili powder, cinnamon, black pepper, and salt and mix well. Cook for another 3 minutes.

When the cooking time for the lentils and rice is complete, let sit for 10 minutes to naturally release the pressure. Turn the steam release handle to the Venting position to release any remaining pressure.

Press Cancel and remove the lid. Mix two-thirds of the onion mixture into the rice and mix well. Taste to see if you need more salt or pepper. Transfer to a serving bowl. Place the remaining onions on top and serve.

LENTILS AND RICE

1 cup (185g) brown rice

½ cup (100g) lentils

2½ cups (591ml) water or Vegetable Stock (see page 44)

¾ teaspoon salt

SPICED ONIONS

3 tablespoons extra virgin olive oil, divided

2 large onions, halved and chopped into ½- to ¾-inch (1.2 to 2cm) pieces

4 cloves garlic, crushed

1 teaspoon turmeric

¼ teaspoon cumin

¼ teaspoon paprika

¼ teaspoon Aleppo or chili powder

¼ teaspoon ground cinnamon

½ teaspoon black pepper

½ teaspoon kosher salt

MOM'S RICE WITH CARAMELIZED ONIONS

GLUTEN-FREE, PARVE, VEGAN

HANDS-ON TIME:	24 Minutes
TIME TO PRESSURE:	8 Minutes
COOKING TIME:	5 Minutes
BUTTONS TO USE:	Sauté and Pressure Cook
NATURAL RELEASE:	Natural Release for 15 Minutes
ADVANCE PREP:	May be made 2 days in advance

Serves 4–6

My mother, Toby Marcus, *z"l*, made this rice almost every Shabbat of my childhood. I remember that she cooked the onions until they were almost black and yet the dish never tasted burnt. Use basic American rice for this recipe rather than fancier basmati or jasmine brands, as they turn out too dry.

3 tablespoons oil

1½ large onions halved and sliced, about 4 heaping cups (1 liter)

1¾ cups (413ml) Vegetable Stock (see page 44)

1 cup (185g) long grain rice

½ teaspoon salt

½ teaspoon black pepper

Press Sauté and when the display reads "Hot," add the oil and onions to the inner pot and cook for 15 to 20 minutes, stirring often, until the onions are browned. After 8 minutes, stir more often to avoid burning. If the onions start to burn, reduce the Sauté level to low or medium by pressing the Sauté button until the light shows the level you want.

Add the stock and stir, using a wooden spoon to scrape up any brown parts on the bottom of the pot. Press Cancel. Add the rice, salt, and pepper and stir. Secure the lid, ensuring that the steam release handle is in the sealing position. Press the Pressure Cook button and set the cooking time for 5 minutes.

When the cooking is complete, let the pot sit to naturally release the pressure for 15 minutes. Turn the steam release handle to the Venting position to release any remaining pressure. Press Cancel. Remove the lid and stir.

VEGETABLE PAELLA

GLUTEN-FREE, PARVE, VEGAN

HANDS-ON TIME:	12 Minutes
TIME TO PRESSURE:	13 Minutes
COOKING TIME:	6 Minutes plus 15 Minutes on Warm after adding the zucchini
BUTTONS TO USE:	Sauté and Pressure Cook
RELEASE TYPE:	Quick Release
ADVANCE PREP:	May be made 1 day in advance

Serves 10 as side dish,
6–8 as the main course

Paella is a Spanish dish typically made with rice, saffron, vegetables, seafood, and sausage. I tasted my first kosher version when my friend Jill Blickstein made one with chicken and kosher spicy sausages. I prefer it as a side dish to serve with any roast chicken or meat, but you can also serve this as a vegetarian main. Another option is to add four sliced vegetarian sausages to the dish when you add the zucchini. The sausages should be cooked first and then sliced and added to the paella when you add the zucchini. Thanks to recipe tester Sarah Feinberg for this inspired addition.

2 tablespoons extra virgin olive oil

1 onion, chopped into ½-inch (1.2cm) pieces

4 cloves garlic, chopped

1 red pepper, cut into ½- to ¾-inch (1.2 to 2cm) pieces

1 green pepper, cut into 1-inch (2.5cm) pieces

1 large fennel bulb, cut into 1-inch (2.5cm) pieces

8 ounces (227g) white mushrooms, halved

1 teaspoon saffron threads

1¾ cups (413ml) Vegetable Stock (see page 44)

Press Sauté and when the display reads "Hot," add the oil, onions, garlic, red and green peppers, and fennel to the inner pot and cook for 4 minutes, stirring occasionally. Add the mushrooms and cook for 2 minutes.

Mix the saffron threads into the stock and set aside. When the vegetables are cooked, add the tomatoes, paprika, salt, pepper, and cayenne pepper and stir. Add the stock and saffron mixture and stir well, using a wooden spoon to scrape the bottom of the pot clean. Add the rice and stir. Press Cancel.

Secure the lid, ensuring that the steam release handle is in the Sealing position. Press the Pressure Cook button and set the cooking time for 6 minutes. When the cooking time is complete, turn the steam release handle to the Venting

ingredients continue on the following page

position to quickly release the pressure. Press Cancel. Remove the lid and stir. Add the peas and carrots and zucchini. Return the lid, press Warm, and let sit for 15 minutes.

2 tomatoes, seeded (see tip on page 21) and chopped into 1-inch (2.5cm) pieces

2 teaspoons smoked paprika

¾ teaspoon salt

½ teaspoon black pepper

pinch or two of cayenne pepper, to taste

1 cup (185g) Arborio rice

1 cup (140g) frozen peas and carrots

1 small zucchini, about 6 ounces (170g), cut into 1-inch (2.5cm) pieces

KASHA VARNISHKES

Kasha, buckwheat, is actually a fruit seed rather than a grain and is related to rhubarb and sorrel. It is a native of China and was brought to Russia in the fourteenth century and then by the Dutch to America. In Russia it was first used as a filling for a pasta, called vareniki, until people got lazy and rather than fill the dough, they simple mixed the kasha with cooked noodles.

In a medium bowl, use a whisk to beat together the egg and the kasha. Press Sauté and when the display reads "Hot," add the coated kasha to the inner pot and cook for 3 minutes, stirring often. Add the stock, pasta, and salt and stir, scraping the bottom clean with a wooden spoon.

Secure the lid, ensuring that the steam release handle is in the Sealing position. Press the Pressure Cook button and set the cooking time for 9 minutes.

Meanwhile, heat the oil in a large frying pan over medium-high heat. Add the onions and let sit for 1 minute, shaking the pan once or twice. Stir and cook for another 10 minutes, stirring often. Turn the heat down after 5 minutes so the onions do not burn. Cook until the onions are well-browned. Add the pepper and stir.

When the cooking time is complete, let sit for 5 minutes to naturally release the pressure. Turn the steam release handle to the Venting position to release any remaining pressure, press Cancel, and remove the lid.

When the kasha and pasta are cooked, place into a bowl. Add the onions and stir. Add salt and pepper as needed.

HANDS-ON TIME: 14 Minutes

TIME TO PRESSURE: 8 Minutes

COOKING TIME: 9 Minutes

BUTTONS TO USE: Sauté and Pressure Cook

RELEASE TYPE: Natural Release for 5 Minutes

ADVANCE PREP: May be made 1 day in advance

Serves 6

1 large egg

1 cup (164g) kasha, medium granulation

3¼ cups (769ml) chicken stock or Vegetable Stock, boiling (see pages 44 and 47)

2 cups (135g) bowtie pasta

½ teaspoon salt

2 tablespoons oil

2 medium onions, sliced

¼ teaspoon black pepper

TZIMMIS

GLUTEN-FREE, PARVE,
PASSOVER, VEGAN

HANDS-ON TIME: 5 Minutes

TIME TO PRESSURE: 12 Minutes

COOKING TIME: 8 Minutes

BUTTON TO USE: Pressure Cook

RELEASE TYPE: Quick Release

ADVANCE PREP: May be made
2 days in advance

Serves 8

It's not Rosh Hashanah or Sukkot without tzimmis, the classic Ashkenazi stew with many variations. When my children were young, I made sure to include on our holiday tables some of the less popular Jewish dishes that are part of our food history so that those recipes would not be lost. For holidays, make sure you include in your menu some of the classic Jewish dishes.

Place the orange juice, stock, sweet potatoes, apricots, prunes, ginger, cinnamon, salt, and pepper into the inner pot. Stir.

Secure the lid, ensuring that the steam release handle is in the Sealing position. Press the Pressure Cook button and set the cooking time for 8 minutes. When the cooking time is complete, turn the steam release handle to the Venting position to quickly release the pressure. Press Cancel and remove the lid. Stir gently and serve.

1 cup (236ml) fresh orange juice, from 3 large oranges

1/2 cup (118ml) chicken stock or Vegetable Stock (see pages 44 and 47)

2 1/2 to 3 pounds (1 to 1.3kg) sweet potatoes, peeled and sliced into 3-inch (7.5cm) chunks

1/2 cup (135g) dried apricots

1/2 cup (135g) pitted prunes

1/4 teaspoon ground ginger

1/2 teaspoon cinnamon

1/2 teaspoon kosher salt

black pepper to taste

POTATO KUGEL

I know what you are thinking—why??!!! It was just a crazy thought, wondering if it could be done. After seeing cake recipes for the IP®, and noodle kugels, it didn't seem so bizarre. The result is a very creamy texture. So yes, if you are making kugel for a huge crowd, you are not making it in the IP®. This recipe serves six, with a nice little wedge of kugel per person. If you know me, you know I am not a kugel chef (with two exceptions), so this is as much kugel as six people truly need. And if you're an empty nester like me, it is perfect!

You will need a 6- or 7-inch (15cm or 18cm) springform pan. Trace the bottom circle on parchment paper and cut out the circle. Cover the top of the pan bottom with aluminum foil and then wrap the foil under the bottom. Attach the pan sides to the bottom and lock and then unwrap the foil and wrap up and around the sides of the pan. Wrap a second piece of foil around the bottom and up the sides of the pan. Pour the oil into the pan. Turn to coat all sides.

Place the onions into a food processor and pulse into small pieces and then process until finely chopped. Remove to a large bowl. Add the potatoes to the processor, pulse into small pieces, and process until finely chopped, almost puréed. Remove to the bowl and add the salt, pepper, sugar, and eggs and mix well.

Pour into the pan. Place the water into the inner pot and add the steam rack. Create an aluminum sling (see page xi). Place the pan on top of the sling and lower onto the rack.

GLUTEN-FREE, PARVE, PASSOVER

HANDS-ON TIME:	5 Minutes
TIME TO PRESSURE:	5 Minutes
COOKING TIME:	40 Minutes, plus 10 Minutes to broil in oven
BUTTON TO USE:	Pressure Cook
RELEASE TYPE:	Quick Release
ADVANCE PREP:	May be made 3 days in advance or frozen

Serves 6

2 tablespoons oil

1 medium onion, cut into quarters

1½ pounds (680g) Yukon gold potatoes, cut into quarters

2 teaspoons salt

heaping ¼ teaspoon black pepper

1 teaspoon sugar

2 large eggs

1 cup (236ml) water

Secure the lid, ensuring that the steam release handle is in the Sealing position. Press the Pressure Cook button and set the cooking time for 40 minutes. When the potato kugel cooking time is complete, turn the steam release handle to the Venting position to quickly release the pressure. Use the sides of the sling to lift the pan out.

Preheat your oven to broil. Remove the foil from the bottom and sides of the pan and place the pan onto a cookie sheet. Broil for 8 to 10 minutes, until browned. Let sit for 5 to 10 minutes and then serve. Remove the sides of the springform pan, separate the parchment from the foil, and move the kugel to a plate to serve.

GARLIC MASHED POTATOES

GLUTEN-FREE, PARVE,
PASSOVER, VEGAN

HANDS-ON TIME: 15 Minutes

TIME TO PRESSURE: 23 Minutes

COOKING TIME: 10 Minutes

BUTTONS TO USE: Pressure Cook

RELEASE TYPE: Quick Release

ADVANCE PREP: May be made 2 days
in advance

Serves 6–8

It doesn't matter what fancy menu I design for major holidays, my four children will always want mashed potatoes alongside every saucy meat dish, while I am more of a rice girl myself. The best potatoes to use for mashed potatoes are the Yukon Gold or Russets. I prefer the Yukon Gold.

3 pounds (1.3kg) Yukon Gold potatoes, peeled and cut into 2-inch (5cm) pieces

5 cups (1.25 liters) water, or enough to cover the potatoes

1 teaspoon kosher salt

¼ cup (59ml) extra virgin olive oil

8 large cloves garlic, crushed

1 large sprig fresh rosemary or 2 sprigs fresh thyme

½ teaspoon fine salt

black pepper to taste

Place the potatoes into the inner pot and add water to cover. Add salt. Secure the lid, ensuring that the steam release handle is in the Sealing position. Press the Pressure Cook button and set the cooking time for 10 minutes.

Meanwhile, place the oil into a small saucepan over low heat. Add the garlic and rosemary and cook until the garlic starts to color, about 6 minutes. Turn off the heat and let it sit until the potatoes are ready.

When the potato cooking time is complete, turn the steam release handle to the Venting position to quickly release the pressure. Press Cancel and remove the lid.

Use a slotted spoon to scoop up half of the potatoes into a large bowl. Do not discard the starchy cooking water. Strain half of the garlic and rosemary oil into the potatoes, without the garlic and rosemary, and use a potato masher to mash together. Repeat for the remaining potatoes and garlic oil and mash. Add 3 tablespoons of the starchy water and mash it in.

Add salt and pepper to taste, and then more salt as needed. Mix well. Reserve 1 cup of the starchy cooking liquid to heat up for serving later. If the potatoes are dry, add the starchy water, a few tablespoons at a time, and mash until smooth. You will not use up all of the starchy water.

MOM'S APPLE RAISIN NOODLE KUGEL

This kugel was on the table every holiday and on the occasional Shabbat in my Long Beach, New York, home growing up. I had forgotten about it until my kids asked for it about a year after their grandma passed away. I couldn't find her recipe, but I recreated it for the IP®. Did you know the noodle kugel comes from twelfth-century Germany?

Trace the bottom of a 7-inch (18cm) round baking pan on parchment paper and cut out a circle. Spray the bottom and sides of the pan with spray oil. Press the parchment circle into the bottom and spray the top of the circle.

Place the noodles and water into the pot and stir. Secure the lid, ensuring that the steam release handle is in the Sealing position. Press the Pressure Cook button and set the cooking time for 1 minute.

While the noodles are cooking, place the eggs, oil, sugar, salt, and cinnamon into a large bowl. Set aside.

When the cooking time is complete, turn the steam release handle to the Venting position to quickly release the pressure. Press Cancel and remove the lid.

Drain the noodles and clean the inner pot. Place the noodles into the large bowl and stir. Return the inner pot to the device; add the steam rack and 1 cup (236ml) of water.

PARVE, VEGETARIAN

NOODLES

HANDS-ON TIME:	3 Minutes
TIME TO PRESSURE:	8 Minutes
COOKING TIME:	1 Minute
BUTTON TO USE:	Pressure Cook
RELEASE TYPE:	Quick Release

KUGEL

HANDS-ON TIME:	5 Minutes
TIME TO PRESSURE:	5 Minutes
COOKING TIME:	24 Minutes
BUTTON TO USE:	Pressure Cook
RELEASE TYPE:	Natural Release for 15 Minutes
ADVANCE PREP:	May be made 2 days in advance or frozen

Serves 6

NOODLES

8 ounces (227g) medium egg noodles

2 cups (473ml) water

KUGEL

spray oil

4 large eggs

1 tablespoon oil

½ cup (100g) sugar

½ teaspoon salt

1 teaspoon cinnamon

2 apples, peeled

1 cup (236ml) water

½ cup (83g) raisins

Cut the apples into ⅓ inch (8mm) cubes, add to the bowl along with the raisins, and mix well. Pour into the prepared pan.

Create an aluminum sling (see page xi). Place the pan on top of the sling and lower onto the rack.

Secure the lid, ensuring that the steam release handle is in the Sealing position. Press the Pressure Cook button and set the cooking time for 24 minutes. When the cooking time is complete, let sit to naturally release the pressure for 15 minutes. While waiting, turn the oven on to broil and take out a cookie sheet.

When the release time has been completed, turn the steam release handle to the Venting position to release any remaining pressure. Press Cancel and remove the lid.

Place the pan on top of the cookie sheet and place it into the oven, but not on the top rack. Broil for 3 to 5 minutes, or until the desired browning has been achieved. Watch carefully so that it does not burn. Place on a cooling rack to cool. Run a knife along the sides of the kugel and flip it onto a plate. Remove the parchment paper from the bottom and transfer to a serving plate.

TOASTING NUTS

On the stovetop: Heat a frying pan over medium heat, add the nuts, and stir often until golden brown on all sides. Watch them very carefully.

In the oven: Preheat the oven to 325°F (162°C). Spread the nuts out on a cookie sheet lined with parchment paper and bake for 15 to 20 minutes, shaking or stirring once or twice, until golden brown and fragrant.

JEWELED ISRAELI COUSCOUS

Israeli couscous, or *ptitim*, as it is called in Israel, was invented in 1953 when Prime Minister David Ben-Gurion asked the local industry to create a wheat-based substitute for rice, which was scarce at the time. It is also called "Ben-Gurion's Rice." In this recipe I prepare it like the Persian rice dish served on special occasions.

Press Sauté, and when the display reads "Hot," add the oil and onions to the inner pot. Cook for 2½ to 3 minutes, stirring often, until the onions start to brown. Add the couscous and cook for another 2 minutes, stirring often. Press Cancel.

Add the stock, saffron, allspice, and salt and stir, scraping the bottom clean with a wooden spoon. Secure the lid, ensuring that the steam release handle is in the Sealing position. Press the Pressure Cook button and set the cooking time for 6 minutes. When the cooking time is complete, let sit for 3 minutes to naturally release the pressure. Turn the steam release handle to the Venting position to release any remaining pressure.

Press Cancel and remove the lid. Add the raisins or barberries, stir, and let sit for 1 minute. Carefully remove the inner pot from the device and add the dill, parsley, cilantro, and pepper. Mix well. Taste and add more salt if needed. Serve garnished with the toasted nuts.

To reheat, add some moisture by adding a tablespoon or two of hot water to the couscous, mix in, and then reheat.

PARVE, VEGAN

HANDS-ON TIME: 10 Minutes

TIME TO PRESSURE: 9 Minutes

COOKING TIME: 6 Minutes

BUTTONS TO USE: Sauté and Pressure Cook

RELEASE TYPE: Natural Release for 3 Minutes

ADVANCE PREP: May be made 2 days in advance

Serves 6

2 tablespoons extra virgin olive oil

1 small onion, chopped into ⅓-inch (8mm) pieces

1 (8.8-ounce [249g]) package of Israeli couscous

2½ cups (591ml) Vegetable Stock (see page 44)

½ teaspoon saffron threads

¼ teaspoon allspice

½ teaspoon salt

½ cup (83g) raisins or ⅓ cup (83g) barberries

½ cup (12g) dill, finely chopped

½ cup (12g) Italian parsley leaves, finely chopped

½ cup (12g) cilantro leaves, finely chopped

⅛ teaspoon black pepper

⅓ cup (38g) slivered almonds, toasted, (see box)

GEORGIAN QUINOA WITH BEETS AND WALNUTS

GLUTEN-FREE, PARVE, PASSOVER, VEGAN

HANDS-ON TIME: 5 Minutes, quinoa and beets need 10 Minutes to cool

TIME TO PRESSURE: 8–9 Minutes

COOKING TIME: 0 Minutes

BUTTON TO USE: Pressure Cook

RELEASE TYPE: Natural Release for 10 Minutes

ADVANCE PREP: May be made 2 days in advance

Serves 6–8

In the summer of 2018, food writer Jessica Halfin took me on a kosher street food tour of Haifa, Israel, and we shot a video of the tour. She took me to bakeries, a bureka place, and a fruit shop. My favorite savory stop was Baribcek, a small restaurant where I tasted this salad. They also serve a sabich bowl of warm hummus, fried eggplant, chickpeas, and tahini that rocked my world. Sabich is a popular Israeli sandwich with fried eggplant, vegetables, hard-boiled egg and tahini.

1 cup (170g) quinoa, rinsed and drained

1½ cups (354ml) water

1 medium beet, peeled and cut into ¼- to ⅓-inch (6mm to 8mm) pieces (wear gloves!)

3 tablespoons extra virgin olive oil

1 stalk celery, chopped into ¼-inch (6mm) pieces

4 green onions, sliced thinly on an angle

⅔ cup (16g) roughly chopped Italian parsley

1 tablespoon lemon juice, from half of 1 lemon

½ teaspoon cumin

¼ teaspoon salt

¼ teaspoon black pepper

1½ cups (150g) walnut halves, chopped roughly

Place the quinoa, water, and beets into the inner pot and stir. Secure the lid, ensuring that the steam release handle is in the Sealing position. Press the Pressure Cook button and set the cooking time for 0 minutes. When the cooking time is complete, let sit for 10 minutes to naturally release the pressure. Turn the steam release handle to the Venting position to release any remaining pressure.

Press Cancel and remove the lid. Stir and then place the quinoa and beets into a large bowl and let cool for at least 10 minutes. Add the oil, celery, green onions, parsley, lemon juice, cumin, salt, pepper, and walnuts. Mix well. Serve at room temperature.

0 MINUTES COOKING TIME

This recipe has a cooking time of zero minutes, as other recipes may indicate as well. In these recipes, the heating process to bring the device to pressure is sufficient to cook the contents.

GARLIC CORN ON THE COB

GLUTEN-FREE, PARVE, VEGAN

HANDS-ON TIME: 3 Minutes

TIME TO PRESSURE: 10 Minutes

COOKING TIME: 3 Minutes

BUTTON TO USE: Pressure Cook

RELEASE TYPE: Quick Release

ADVANCE PREP: May be made 2 days in advance

Serves 4,
may cook up to 6

I grew up eating corn on the cob with salt and margarine or butter and never imagined it could be served any other way. As I have traveled as an adult, I have eaten corn slathered with many different toppings, including once with grated cheese and soy sauce, an unusual pairing. Here is a simple recipe, but you can also add chili powder to make it spicier, flavored butter, or even an Asian marinade.

1 cup (236ml) water

4 ears corn on the cob, shucked, broken in half or left whole

2 tablespoons extra virgin olive oil

2 cloves garlic, crushed

¼ teaspoon kosher salt

black pepper to taste

Place the water into the inner pot and insert the steam rack. Place the cobs on top of the rack.

Secure the lid, ensuring that the steam release handle is in the Sealing position. Press the Pressure Cook button and set the cooking time for 3 minutes.

While the corn is cooking, place the oil, garlic, salt, and pepper into a small bowl and mix well.

When the cooking time is complete, turn the steam release handle to the Venting position to quickly release the pressure. Press Cancel and remove the lid.

Remove the corn carefully to a serving platter. Brush the garlic mixture all over the cobs and serve.

RATATOUILLE

Ratatouille is a classic French Provençale dish and it will always remind me of the years Andy and I lived in Geneva, Switzerland. Geneva is surrounded on all sides by France, and we took many car trips down to Provence, exploring different towns every time. We even found a few charming old synagogues to visit.

Press Sauté and when the display reads "Hot," add the oil and onions to the inner pot and cook for 3 minutes. Add the eggplant and cook, stirring often, for 5 minutes. Add the pepper and zucchini and cook for another 2 minutes. Add the garlic, tomato, tomato paste, water, salt, and pepper. Stir.

Secure the lid, ensuring that the steam release handle is in the Sealing position. Press the Pressure Cook button and set the cooking time for 2 minutes. When the cooking time is complete, turn the steam release handle to the Venting position to quickly release the pressure. Remove the lid.

Add two-thirds of the basil leaves and the capers to the pot and stir. Return the lid and let sit on Warm for 5 minutes. When ready to serve, sprinkle the remaining basil leaves on top.

GLUTEN-FREE, PARVE, PASSOVER, VEGAN

HANDS-ON TIME: 14 Minutes

TIME TO PRESSURE: 10 Minutes

COOKING TIME: 2 Minutes, plus 5 Minutes on Warm

BUTTONS TO USE: Sauté and Pressure Cook

RELEASE TYPE: Quick Release

ADVANCE PREP: May be made 2 days in advance

Serves 6–8

2 tablespoons extra virgin olive oil

1 onion, chopped into ½-inch (1.2cm) pieces

1 large eggplant, unpeeled, cut into 1-inch (2.5cm) pieces

1 red pepper, cut into 1½-inch (4cm) pieces

1 large zucchini, unpeeled, cut into ½-inch (1.2cm) pieces

4 cloves garlic, roughly chopped

1 large fresh tomato, seeded and chopped into 1-inch (2.5cm) pieces

2 tablespoons tomato paste

¼ cup (59ml) water

½ teaspoon salt

¼ teaspoon black pepper

6 fresh basil leaves, chiffonade, (see page 124), divided

1 tablespoon capers, drained

SPAGHETTI SQUASH WITH FRESH CHERRY TOMATO SAUCE

I try very hard not to waste produce. This recipe was created when I had dying cherry tomatoes in my fridge that needed to be used up. Try to find ways to cook ingredients you already have before going out to buy more. I realize that this recipe has a step outside of the IP®, but my goal was to have the sauce ready by the time the squash was cooked.

Place the water into the inner pot and insert the steam rack. Place the squash halves on top of the rack.

Secure the lid, ensuring that the steam release handle is in the Sealing position. Press the Pressure Cook button and set the cooking time for 9 minutes.

Meanwhile, in large frying pan, heat the oil over medium heat. Add the garlic and cook for 1 minute, or until a few pieces start to color. Add the tomatoes and continue cooking for 7 to 9 minutes, or until most of the tomatoes break down and you have a sauce. Stir occasionally. The mixture should bubble the entire time. Add the salt and pepper and turn off the heat.

When the squash cooking time is complete, turn the steam release handle to the Venting position to quickly release the pressure. Press Cancel and remove the lid.

GLUTEN-FREE, PARVE, PASSOVER, VEGAN

HANDS-ON TIME: 15 Minutes
TIME TO PRESSURE: 6 Minutes
COOKING TIME: 9 Minutes
BUTTON TO USE: Pressure Cook
RELEASE TYPE: Quick Release
ADVANCE PREP: May be made 2 days in advance

Serves 6–8

1 cup (236ml) water

1 spaghetti squash, about 2½ pounds (1kg), cut in half horizontally and seeds scooped out

1 tablespoon extra-virgin olive oil

3 large cloves garlic, finely minced

2 pounds (907g) cherry tomatoes, different colors preferably, halved the long way

¼ teaspoon kosher salt

generous pinch Aleppo pepper or freshly ground black pepper

Use a large fork to lift up the squash halves into a colander and let cool for 2 minutes, or until you can handle them; I lift them with a dishtowel. Use the fork to scrape the threads of the squash into the frying pan. Turn the sauce back on to medium heat. Use a fork to mix the squash into the sauce. When it is all mixed in, cook for 2 minutes. Taste and add more salt if needed.

CAULIFLOWER PURÉE

GLUTEN-FREE, PARVE,
PASSOVER, VEGAN

HANDS-ON TIME: 7 Minutes

TIME TO PRESSURE: 18 Minutes

COOKING TIME: 5 Minutes

BUTTONS TO USE: Sauté and Pressure Cook

RELEASE TYPE: Quick Release

ADVANCE PREP: May be made 2 days in advance

Serves 8

This is a healthy alternative to mashed potatoes. I had this recipe tested by Barbara Libbin, a health coach with Optavia, who lost 50 pounds (23kg) and went on to inspire many others, including my husband, to meet their weight loss goals. When developing menus, you should always try to balance out some of the heavier dishes with some lighter ones.

2 tablespoons extra virgin olive oil

1 large onion, chopped into 1-inch (2.5cm) pieces

1 shallot, sliced

3 cloves garlic, chopped roughly

1 large parsnip, cut into 1-inch (2.5cm) pieces

1 large head cauliflower, cut into 3-inch (8cm) pieces

1 cup (236ml) water

¾ teaspoon salt

2 pinches white pepper

Press Sauté and when the display reads "Hot," add the oil, onions, shallots, and garlic to the inner pot and cook for 3 minutes, stirring often. Add the parsnip, cauliflower, and water and stir, scraping the bottom well with a wooden spoon.

Secure the lid, ensuring that the steam release handle is in the Sealing position. Press the Pressure Cook button and set the cooking time for 5 minutes. When the cooking time is complete, turn the steam release handle to the Venting position to quickly release the pressure. Press Cancel and remove the lid.

Drain the cauliflower over a bowl, gently press out the liquid, and reserve the cooking liquid.

Place the cauliflower into a food processor, blender, or bowl to use with an immersion blender. Purée until smooth, and add some cooking liquid, 1 tablespoon at a time, as needed to create a creamy but not too liquidy texture. Add the salt and white pepper and mix well.

CRANBERRY AND ORANGE SAUCE

GLUTEN-FREE, PARVE,
PASSOVER, VEGAN

HANDS-ON TIME: 2 Minutes, needs to cool for 2 hours and then chill for 4 hours

TIME TO PRESSURE: 14 Minutes

COOKING TIME: 2 Minutes

BUTTON TO USE: Pressure Cook

RELEASE TYPE: Quick Release

ADVANCE PREP: May be made 4 days in advance

Makes 1½ cups (354ml) sauce, enough for a huge turkey

Thanksgiving is my favorite holiday as I just love all the holiday flavors. When I was pregnant with my twins, who are now 20 years old, I was on bed rest for Thanksgiving 1999. I was allowed to come down the stairs once a day, and I was beached on the sofa during the meal prep. From there I directed my husband Andy and his cousin Carol Auerbach to prepare the meal. Andy was tasked with the cranberry sauce, and he had never zested citrus before. I am guessing that all he imagined was cocktails with an orange peel so he cut large pieces of peel and added them to the cranberry sauce. I have to admit that everyone agreed that the sauce was very tasty, but you just couldn't eat the peels. I learned that you have to give people really specific instructions. Here is a new version of that recipe.

16 ounces (454g) fresh or frozen cranberries

1 cup (236ml) cranberry juice

½ cup (80g) dried cranberries

½ cup (100g) sugar

3 tablespoons apricot preserves

2 teaspoons orange zest, from 1 orange

3 tablespoons orange juice, from zested orange

¼ teaspoon nutmeg

¼ teaspoon cinnamon

Place the cranberries, cranberry juice, dried cranberries, and sugar into the inner pot and stir. Secure the lid, ensuring that the steam release handle is in the Sealing position. Press the Pressure Cook button and set the cooking time for 2 minutes.

When the cooking time is complete, turn the steam release handle to the Venting position to quickly release the pressure. Remove the lid.

Add the apricot preserves, orange zest and juice, nutmeg, and cinnamon and stir. Use a potato masher to mash the sauce, leaving just a few cranberries whole. Press Cancel.

Let the pot sit in the device for 2 hours to cool. Place in a container and chill in the fridge for at least 4 hours to thicken.

ASPARAGUS WITH LEMON AND HERB SAUCE

This recipe works best with the thicker asparagus spears, as the thin ones will be reduced to mush.

Place 1 cup (236ml) of water into the inner pot and insert the steam rack. Stack the asparagus spears on top, placing them in different directions.

Secure the lid, ensuring that the steam release handle is in the Sealing position. Press the Pressure Cook button and set the cooking time for 0 minutes.

Meanwhile, make the sauce. Place the basil, parsley, capers, lemon juice, mustard, and garlic into a blender or food processor and process until chopped. Add the oil, 2 tablespoons of water, salt, and pepper and process, scraping down the sides of the bowl a few times and processing some more, until you have a thick, creamy sauce.

When the cooking time is complete, turn the steam release handle to the Venting position to quickly release the pressure. Press Cancel and remove the lid.

Remove the asparagus to a large colander and rinse with cold water. Dry and place on a serving platter.

Drizzle the sauce on top of the asparagus, a little at a time, and toss to coat. Serve at room temperature.

GLUTEN-FREE, PARVE, VEGAN

HANDS-ON TIME:	4 Minutes
TIME TO PRESSURE:	9 Minutes
COOKING TIME:	0 Minutes
BUTTON TO USE:	Pressure Cook
RELEASE TYPE:	Quick Release
ADVANCE PREP:	May be made 2 days in advance

Serves 6

ASPARAGUS

1 cup (236ml) water

2 pounds (907g) thick asparagus, trimmed and bottom third peeled with a vegetable peeler

SAUCE

10 large basil leaves

½ cup (12g) Italian parsley leaves

1½ tablespoons capers, drained and rinsed

1 tablespoon fresh lemon juice, from 1 lemon

2 teaspoons Dijon mustard

1 clove garlic

2 tablespoons extra virgin olive oil

2 tablespoons water

¼ teaspoon fine salt

black pepper to taste

DESSERTS

HONEY CAKE WITH COFFEE AND HONEY GLAZE

It's not Rosh Hashanah without honey cake and even I, The Kosher Baker, was surprised with how moist this cake was. Japanese and Chinese bakers have steamed cakes for centuries.

Spray a 6- or 7-inch (15cm or 18cm) round pan with oil and set aside. Place the water into the inner pot and insert the steam rack.

In a medium bowl place the hot coffee, honey, oil, and brown sugar and whisk well. Add the eggs and mix in. Add the flour, cloves, ginger, cinnamon, baking powder, baking soda, and salt and mix well. Pour into the prepared pan. Take a piece of aluminum foil large enough to cover the pan and spray oil on one side. Cover the pan with the greased side facing the cake batter. Cover tightly. Create an aluminum foil sling (see page xi). Place the pan on top of the foil.

Lift the sides of the foil to place the pan onto the rack. Secure the lid, ensuring that the steam release handle is in the Sealing position. Press the Pressure Cook button and set the cooking time for 40 minutes.

When the cooking time is complete, let sit for 15 minutes to naturally release the pressure. Turn the steam release handle to the Venting position to release any remaining pressure. Press

PARVE

HANDS-ON TIME:	5 Minutes, plus cooling time
TIME TO PRESSURE:	7 Minutes
COOKING TIME:	40 Minutes
BUTTON TO USE:	Pressure Cook
RELEASE TYPE:	Natural Release for 15 Minutes
ADVANCE PREP:	May be made 3 days in advance or frozen

Serves 6–8

CAKE

spray oil to grease pan

1 cup (236ml) water

½ cup (118ml) prepared strong coffee or espresso

½ cup (118ml) honey

⅓ cup (79ml) oil

3 tablespoons dark brown sugar

2 large eggs

1¼ cups (140g) all-purpose flour

¼ teaspoon cloves

¼ teaspoon ginger

¼ teaspoon cinnamon

½ teaspoon baking powder

¼ teaspoon baking soda

¼ teaspoon salt

ingredients continue on the following page

Cancel. Use the sides of the sling to lift up the cake and remove to a cooling rack. Let cool for 10 minutes and then turn the cake out of the pan onto the cooling rack to cool completely.

While the cake is cooling prepare the glaze. Place the confectioners' sugar into a bowl. Add the coffee and honey and whisk well. Let sit for 5 minutes to thicken. Either spread the glaze on top or use a whisk to drizzle lines over the cake.

GLAZE

½ cup (63g) confectioners' sugar

2 teaspoons prepared hot espresso or coffee

½ teaspoon honey

SPONGE CAKE

My grandmother's sponge cake kept her young. She lived to age 98 on a steady diet of sponge cake and Sanka, and I recall that she continued baking this cake until she was at least 90 years old. I thought there was some magic to her recipe, but one day my aunt found a photocopy of the side of the Streit's cake meal box that had a sponge cake recipe on it with grandma's many handwritten variations. Here is my IP® version.

Place the egg yolks, 1½ tablespoons water, lemon zest, juice, and ½ cup (100g) of the sugar into a medium bowl and whisk well. Add the potato starch and whisk well. Place the egg whites into a large mixing bowl. With an electric mixer, start beating on low speed and when foamy add the salt and mix. Turn the speed up to high and beat until you have soft peaks. Turn the speed down to low and add 2 tablespoons (25g) of sugar, a little at a time. When the sugar is all mixed in, turn the speed up to high for 1 minute. Scoop up one-third of the whites and whisk into the lemon mixture. Add another third and mix in more slowly than the first. Add the remaining whites and mix in gently.

Pour the batter into an ungreased 7-inch (18cm) tube pan. Use a silcone spatula to smooth the top. Cover the pan with aluminum foil. Place 1 cup of water and the steam rack into the inner pot. Create an aluminum foil sling (see page xi). Place the pan on top of the foil. Lift the sides of the foil to place the pan onto the rack.

GLUTEN-FREE, PARVE, PASSOVER

HANDS-ON TIME:	5 Minutes, plus cooling time
TIME TO PRESSURE:	6 Minutes
COOKING TIME:	27 Minutes
BUTTON TO USE:	Pressure Cook
RELEASE TYPE:	Natural Release for 10 Minutes
ADVANCE PREP:	May be made 3 days in advance or frozen

Serves 6–8

3 large eggs, separated

1 cup (236ml) plus 1½ tablespoons water, divided

2 teaspoons zest, from 1 lemon

4 teaspoons lemon juice, from 1 lemon

½ cup (100g) plus 2 tablespoons (25g) sugar, divided

⅓ cup (56g) potato starch

⅛ teaspoon salt

Secure the lid, ensuring that the steam release handle is in the Sealing position. Press the Pressure Cook button and set the cooking time for 27 minutes. When the cooking time is complete, let sit for 10 minutes to naturally release the pressure. Turn the steam release handle to the Venting position to release any remaining pressure.

Carefully lift the foil sides to remove the pan from the pot and let cool; the cake will pull away from the sides of the pan while it cools. If not, then gently use your fingers to pull the cake away from the sides and then turn onto a cooling rack or serving plate.

APPLESAUCE

GLUTEN-FREE, PARVE,
PASSOVER

HANDS-ON TIME: 8 Minutes

TIME TO PRESSURE: 4 Minutes

COOKING TIME: 5 Minutes

BUTTON TO USE: Pressure Cook

RELEASE TYPE: Natural Release for
5 Minutes

ADVANCE PREP: May be made 2 days
in advance

This is one of those basic Jewish recipes that can be used as a side dish, dessert, or snack. I typically like to mix types of apples and include some sweeter ones, such as one or two Red Delicious ones, as I do not add sugar to my recipe.

Makes 4½ cups (1 liter)

4 pounds (1.8kg) apples, mixed types, about 8 large, peeled and cut into 2-inch (5cm) pieces

1 teaspoon chopped ginger

1 cinnamon stick

⅓ cup (79ml) water

Place the apples, ginger, cinnamon stick, and water into the inner pot. Secure the lid, ensuring that the steam release handle is in the Sealing position. Press the Pressure Cook button and set the cooking time for 5 minutes. When the cooking time is complete, let the pot sit for 5 minutes to naturally release the pressure.

Turn the steam release handle to the Venting position to release any remaining pressure. Press Cancel and remove the lid. Remove the cinnamon stick and partially purée the apples with an immersion blender for a few seconds, leaving some pieces whole.

MOCHA
LAVA CAKES

Lava cakes are probably one of the most popular desserts served at events I attend. Everyone loves the cake outside and gooey inside. Because most recipes are designed for the cakes to be eaten very soon after they come out of the oven, lava cakes aren't Shabbat-friendly. Purely by accident I created these. I unmolded one and found it much too gooey, which meant I had to test it again. I left the others on my counter and unmolded them after dinner, many hours later, and found the texture perfect. So make these before Shabbat and enjoy them for dessert or make in advance of any dinner party or event.

You will need six 6-ounce (175ml) ramekins. Place the chocolate and coconut oil into a heatproof bowl and microwave for 1 minute, stir, and then melt for another 45 seconds, stir, and then for 30 seconds if needed, until melted. Add the instant coffee, vanilla, and cocoa and whisk in.

Place the eggs, egg yolks, and sugar into a large mixing bowl. Use an electric mixer to mix at low speed to combine and then turn the speed up to high and beat for 3 minutes. Add the potato starch and beat at low speed to just combine. Add the melted chocolate mixture and whisk gently until combined.

Spray the ramekins with spray oil. Divide the batter among the prepared ramekins, a heaping ½ cup (118ml) for each mold.

DAIRY OR PARVE,
GLUTEN-FREE, PASSOVER

HANDS-ON TIME: 12 Minutes to cook in batches , plus 30 Minutes to cool

TIME TO PRESSURE: 7 Minutes

COOKING TIME: 7 Minutes

BUTTON TO USE: Pressure Cook

RELEASE TYPE: Quick Release

ADVANCE PREP: May be made 4 hours in advance

Serves 6

7 ounces (198g) bittersweet chocolate, chopped

½ cup (118ml) coconut oil, margarine, or butter

2 tablespoons plus 1 teaspoon instant coffee granules

2 teaspoons pure vanilla extract

1 tablespoon unsweetened cocoa

2 large eggs plus 2 yolks

½ cup (100g) sugar

⅓ cup (56g) potato starch

spray oil

1 cup (236ml) plus 2 tablespoons water, divided

Place the water into the inner pot and insert the steam rack. Place three of the ramekins in a circle around the rack.

Secure the lid, ensuring that the steam release handle is in the Sealing position. Press the Pressure Cook button and set the cooking time for 7 minutes. When the cooking time is complete, press Cancel. Turn the steam release handle to the Venting position to quickly release the pressure.

Carefully remove the ramekins from the pot. Add another 2 tablespoons of water to the pot and cook the remaining three cakes as you did the first batch. It will take about 2 minutes for the Instant Pot® to return to pressure.

Let the cakes cool for at least 30 minutes before unmolding. To unmold, run a thin knife or small metal spatula around the edge of the cake, place a plate on top, and turn the cake onto the plate. Dust with confectioners' sugar if desired and serve with fruit.

MELTING CHOCOLATE

Place chocolate chopped into ½-inch (1.2cm) pieces into a microwave-safe bowl, such as a large glass bowl. Make sure you have discarded every tiny piece of foil that wrapped the chocolate. Heat for 1 minute at high power, or 45 seconds to start if you have less than 10 ounces (238g) of chocolate. Remove the bowl from the microwave and stir well, mixing the melted pieces into the unmelted ones for about 30 seconds. Heat for another 45 or 30 seconds and stir again for about 1 minute. If the chocolate is not fully melted, heat for another 30 seconds and stir. Repeat for 15 seconds if necessary. Be sure to have oven mitts on hand to hold the bowl when you stir it.

FLOURLESS CHOCOLATE CAKE

DAIRY OR PARVE, GLUTEN-FREE, PASSOVER

HANDS-ON TIME: 8 Minutes, let cool for 30 Minutes and then chill for 8 hours

TIME TO PRESSURE: 5 Minutes

COOKING TIME: 18 Minutes

BUTTON TO USE: Pressure Cook

RELEASE TYPE: Natural Release for 10 Minutes

ADVANCE PREP: May be made 2 days in advance or frozen

Serves 6–8

Flourless chocolate cake is the dessert that everyone should have in his or her baking arsenal. It has five ingredients that I always have on hand, as I buy good quality parve chocolate in bulk. It is a Passover favorite and because it is gluten-free, it can be served to people with that allergy or sensitivity. It is also very rich, so the mini IP® size is great for portion control.

Take a 7-inch (18cm) springform pan, place it on top of a piece of parchment paper on your counter, and trace a circle around the bottom of the pan. Cut out the circle and set aside. Place a large piece of foil on top of the bottom of the pan and fold the excess foil under the pan. Attach the sides of the pan, lock in place, and then take the part of the foil that you folded under the pan and wrap it up the sides of the pan.

Grease the top of the foil in the bottom of the pan. Place the parchment circle on top and press the circle into the bottom of the pan on top of the foil. This step makes it easy to slide the finished cake onto your serving plate. Grease the parchment circle and the sides of the pan.

Place the chocolate and butter, margarine, or coconut oil into a heatproof bowl and melt in the microwave for 1 minute, stir, heat for another 45 seconds, stir, and add more time as needed until melted. When the chocolate is melted, add the egg yolks and cocoa and whisk well.

6 tablespoons (84g) butter, margarine, or coconut oil, plus 1 tablespoon (14g) for greasing the pan

8 ounces (227g) bittersweet chocolate, chopped roughly

6 large eggs, separated

2 teaspoons unsweetened cocoa

½ cup (100g) sugar

1 cup (236ml) water

In a separate bowl, beat the egg whites with an electric mixer until stiff. Turn the speed down to low, add the sugar slowly, and once all the sugar is added, turn the speed up to high for 1 minute.

Fold the egg whites into the chocolate mixture. Pour the batter into the prepared pan. Place 1 cup (236ml) of water into the inner pot and insert the steam rack. Create an aluminum foil sling (see page xi). Place the cake on top of the sling and use the sides to lift up the cake and place it on top of the steam rack. Fold the top of the sling over the top of the pan.

Secure the lid, ensuring that the steam release handle is in the Sealing position. Press the Pressure Cook button and set the time for 18 minutes. When the cooking time is complete, let the pot sit for 10 minutes to naturally release the pressure. Turn the steam release handle to the Venting position to release any remaining pressure. Use the sides of the sling to lift up the cake and remove to a rack. Let cool for 30 minutes. Place into a fridge for 8 hours or overnight.

Unlock the pan and remove the sides. Use a metal spatula to separate the parchment from the cake bottom and move the cake to a plate. Heat a large knife to slice the cake.

BEATING EGG WHITES

Whip the egg whites on medium speed until foamy, and then reduce the speed to low and add a pinch of salt or few drops of lemon juice, according to the recipe. Return the speed to medium for a few seconds, and then increase it to high. Soft peaks bend slightly when you gently lift up the whisk or beater. If your recipe requires stiff peaks, then beat until the peak stands straight up when you lift the beaters.

NEW YORK CHEESECAKE WITH ORANGE CARAMEL SAUCE

Cheesecake is one of my favorite desserts, and as it is very addictive, making a smaller one in the IP® is really helpful to make sure I cannot eat too much. The caramel sauce makes it even more decadent, but it is optional. This can be made gluten-free with gluten-free cookies and a flour substitute.

You will need a 6- or 7-inch (15cm or 18cm) springform pan. Trace the bottom circle on parchment paper and cut out the circle. Place a large piece of foil on top of the pan bottom and fold the excess foil under the pan bottom. Attach the outer section of the pan, lock it in place, and then take the part of the foil that you folded under the pan and wrap it up and around the outside of the pan. Take the unmelted tablespoon of butter and rub around the bottom and sides of the pan. Press the parchment circle into the bottom and grease the top of the circle.

Place the cookies into the bowl of a food processor fitted with a metal blade and process until ground, but not completely in crumbs; leave some ¼-inch pieces. Add the melted butter and pulse a few seconds to mix. Scoop into the pan and press to cover the bottom. Set aside.

To make the filling, place the cream cheese into a mixing bowl and beat with an electric mixer until creamy. Add the

DAIRY, GLUTEN-FREE
(WITH SUBSTITUTIONS)

HANDS-ON TIME:	12 Minutes, cake needs to cool for 30 Minutes then chill for 6 hours
TIME TO PRESSURE:	5 Minutes
COOKING TIME:	30 Minutes
BUTTON TO USE:	Pressure Cook
RELEASE TYPE:	Natural for 10 Minutes
ADVANCE PREP:	Cake may be made 2 days in advance or frozen

Serves 6–8

CRUST

4 tablespoons (56g) unsalted butter, melted for about 30 seconds in the microwave, plus 1 tablespoon (14g) butter, not melted, for greasing pan

4 ounces (113g) shortbread cookies or gluten-free vanilla cookies

FILLING

16 ounces (454g) cream cheese, at room temperature

3 large eggs

½ cup (100g) sugar

1 teaspoon lemon zest, from 1 lemon

ingredients continue on the following page

eggs, one at a time, and beat well, scraping down the bowl a few times. Add the sugar, zests, vanilla, and flour and mix well.

Place the 1 cup (236ml) of water into the inner pot and insert the steam rack. Create an aluminum foil sling (see page xi). Place the pan on top of the sling and then lift the sides to insert onto the steam rack. Fold the top of the sling over the top of the pan. Secure the lid, ensuring that the steam release handle is in the Sealing position. Press the Pressure Cook button and set the cooking time for 30 minutes.

Meanwhile, prepare the caramel. Place the sugar and water in a small, heavy-bottomed saucepan. Cook on medium-high heat until the sugar melts without stirring. After several minutes, the sugar will color, and then you will stir to mix all the sugar together. Continue cooking, stirring often until you have an amber color. Reduce heat to low, remove the saucepan from the heat, and add the cream. Be careful, as the mixture will bubble up. Add the butter and orange juice and stir. Return to the heat and cook for 1 minute, or until the mixture is smooth, stirring often. Remove from heat. Let cool. Store in the fridge.

When the cheesecake cooking time is complete, let sit for 10 minutes to naturally release the pressure. Turn the steam release handle to the Venting position to release any remaining pressure. Press Cancel. Remove the lid and then lift the sides of the sling to remove the pan. Let cool at room temperature for 30 minutes. Place into the fridge for 6 hours or overnight. Unlock the pan and remove the sides. Use a metal spatula to separate the parchment from the cake bottom and move the cake to a plate.

Serve sliced with the caramel sauce on top or alongside. The sauce can also be reheated.

1 teaspoon orange zest, from 1 orange

1 teaspoon pure vanilla extract

1 tablespoon all-purpose flour or gluten-free flour

1 cup (236ml) water

CARAMEL

¾ cup (150g) sugar

2 tablespoons water

⅓ cup (79ml) whipping cream

2 tablespoons (28g) butter

2 tablespoons fresh orange juice, from zested orange

BERRY COMPOTE

This recipe is delicious on its own, served in bowls, or as a sauce or topping for the Lemon Labne Pots de Crème (see page 188), the Flourless Chocolate Cake (see page 182), or the Sponge Cake (see page 176). For this dish you need a 6- or 7-inch (15cm or 18cm) ceramic soufflé dish, with higher sides than a round baking pan, because of the volume of berries.

Place the berries into a soufflé dish that fits inside your Instant Pot®. Add the sugar, lemon juice, cornstarch, and vanilla and stir until you do not see any sugar or cornstarch. Place the water inside the inner pot and insert the steam rack. Create an aluminum foil sling (see page xi). Place the dish on top of the foil and lift the sides to place the dish inside the pot on top of the steam rack.

Secure the lid, ensuring that the steam release handle is in the Sealing position. Press the Pressure Cook button and set the cooking time for 5 minutes.

When the cooking time is complete, let sit for 10 minutes to naturally release the pressure. Turn the steam release handle to the Venting position to release any remaining pressure. Press Cancel and remove the lid.

Use a potato masher to smash some of the berries. Lift the sides of the foil to lift the dish from the pot. Let sit for 1 hour to cool and thicken.

GLUTEN-FREE, PARVE

HANDS-ON TIME: 7 Minutes, compote must sit for 1 hour to thicken

TIME TO PRESSURE: 5 Minutes

COOKING TIME: 5 Minutes

BUTTON TO USE: Pressure Cook

RELEASE TYPE: Natural Release for 10 Minutes

ADVANCE PREP: May be made 2 days in advance

Serves 6

8 cups (1.2kg) mixed blueberries, blackberries, and raspberries; you can also add some plums chopped into ½-inch (1.2cm) pieces, so long as the total is 8 cups (2 liters) of fruit

¾ cup (150g) sugar

1 tablespoon lemon juice from 1 lemon

¼ cup (32g) cornstarch

2 teaspoons pure vanilla extract

1 cup (236ml) water

LEMON LABNE POTS DE CRÈME

GLUTEN-FREE, DAIRY

HANDS-ON TIME:	10 Minutes, plus 30 Minutes cooling time, then chill for at least 4 hours
TIME TO PRESSURE:	8 Minutes
COOKING TIME:	7 Minutes
BUTTON TO USE:	Pressure Cook
RELEASE TYPE:	Natural Release for 15 Minutes

This recipe makes six small, lemony custards that are perfect with fresh berries or the Berry Compote on page 187.

Serves 6

2 cups (473ml) water

2 cups (473ml) heavy cream

¾ cup (150g) sugar, divided

6 large egg yolks

1 teaspoon lemon zest, from 1 lemon

3 tablespoons fresh lemon juice, from 2 lemons

1 tablespoon cornstarch

⅓ cup (78ml) labne or yogurt

Place the water into the inner pot and place the steam rack inside. You will need six 6-ounce (175ml) ceramic ramekins for this recipe.

Place the cream and half of the sugar into a small saucepan and heat over low heat. Stir occasionally. Meanwhile, in a medium bowl, place the egg yolks, lemon zest, lemon juice, cornstarch, and remaining sugar and whisk well. When you see small bubbles in the cream mixture, after about 4 to 5 minutes, remove from the heat and pour a little into the bowl with the egg yolk mixture. Whisk well. Add half of the remaining cream mixture and whisk. Add the remaining cream mixture and whisk in. Add the labne or yogurt and whisk well. Strain into another bowl and press as much liquid as possible through the sieve.

Divide the batter among the ramekins, about ½ cup (118ml) of the batter in each. Cover each ramekin with a small piece of aluminum foil. Place 3 ramekins onto the steam rack and then stack the other 3 on top.

Secure the lid, ensuring that the steam release handle is in the Sealing position. Press the Pressure Cook button and set the cooking time for 7 minutes. When the cooking time is complete, let the pot sit to naturally release the pressure, for 15 minutes. Turn the steam release handle to the Venting position to release any remaining pressure. Remove the lid. Carefully remove the ramekins to the counter and let cool for 30 minutes. Refrigerate for at least 4 hours or overnight, until firm.

MALABI-INSPIRED FLAN

Malabi is a rose-flavored milk pudding popular in Israel and all over the Middle East. Its origin is Persian, though the first written recipe came from Iraq. In this recipe, I married this classic Israeli dessert with a Latin American cream cheese flan.

To make the flan caramel, place the sugar and water into a small, heavy-bottomed saucepan. Do not mix. Cook on medium-high heat and let sit until the sugar starts to color around the edges. Use a wooden spoon to push the colored edges into the center and stir to mix the unmelted sugar into the melted part. Continue cooking, stirring often, until all of the sugar pieces have melted. When the melted sugar is a uniform amber color, remove the saucepan from the heat.

Carefully pour the caramel into a 7-inch (18cm) round pan and swirl around three times so the caramel coats 1 to 2 inches (2.5 to 5cm) up the sides of the pan. Set aside.

Place the eggs, cream cheese, milk, condensed milk, and rosewater into a blender and mix at high speed for 1 minute until it is completely smooth. Pour over the caramel in the pan. Cover with aluminum foil.

Create an aluminum foil sling (see page xi). Place the pan on top of the sling. Place 1½ cups (354ml) of water into the inner pot and insert the steam rack. Use the sides of the sling to lift the pan and place on top of the rack. Fold the top of the sling over the top of the pan.

DAIRY, GLUTEN-FREE

HANDS-ON TIME: 12 Minutes, let cool at room temperature for 1 hour and chill for 8 hours before serving

TIME TO PRESSURE: 6 Minutes

COOKING TIME: 40 Minutes

BUTTON TO USE: Pressure Cook

RELEASE TYPE: Natural Release for 30 Minutes

ADVANCE PREP: Flan or sauce may be made 2 days in advance

Serves 6–8

FLAN

¾ cup (150g) sugar

1 teaspoon water

6 large eggs

4 ounces (113g) cream cheese

¼ cup (59ml) whole milk

½ of a 14-ounce (414ml) can sweetened condensed milk

2 tablespoons rosewater

1½ cups (354ml) water

RASPBERRY AND ROSE SAUCE

2 cups (250g) fresh raspberries

¼ cup (59ml) hot water

2 tablespoons confectioners' sugar, or more to taste

1 tablespoon rosewater

Secure the lid, ensuring that the steam release handle is in the Sealing position. Press the Pressure Cook button and set the cooking time for 40 minutes.

When the cooking time is complete, let the pot sit for 30 minutes to naturally release the pressure. Turn the steam release handle to the Venting position. Press Cancel. Remove the lid and use the sides of the sling to carefully lift up the flan. Remove the foil cover and let cool to room temperature for at least 1 hour.

Meanwhile, place the raspberries, hot water, and confectioners' sugar into a food processor or blender and process until smooth. Taste and add more confectioners' sugar if desired. Strain the mixture into a small serving bowl. Add the rosewater and stir. The sauce may be made 2 days in advance and stored in the fridge.

When the flan has cooled, run a thin knife along the sides of the dish to release the flan from the sides. Place a pie pan or platter with a rim over the top of the flan pan and turn the flan over onto it, letting the caramel drip over the sides. If any of the caramel is stuck to the bottom of the pan, let the pan sit in a larger pan of hot water for a few minutes to release the caramel, and pour it over the flan. Cover the flan with plastic and place in the fridge for at least 8 hours or overnight.

To serve, pour some of the sauce over the top of the flan and spread to cover. You can serve the remaining sauce alongside.

STRAINING SEEDED FRUIT

Whenever I make a berry sauce, after I purée the fruit in a food processor or blender, I strain it through a sieve and discard the seeds so that the sauce is completely smooth.

GRANDMA'S RICE PUDDING

This was one of my Grandma Sylvia's specialties. I remember eating it at her apartment in Florida for the first time around age 12 and thinking that I had never eaten anything so luscious. Every rice pudding I have tasted since has never measured up. Grandma added yellow raisins to her rice pudding, but I prefer the classic taste.

Place the rice and water into the inner pot. Secure the lid, ensuring that the steam release handle is in the Sealing position. Press the Rice button to cook the rice. When the cooking time is complete, let the pot sit for 15 minutes or more to fully release the pressure. Turn the steam release handle to the Venting position. Press Cancel. Remove the lid and use a wooden spoon to stir the rice.

Add the milk, brown sugar, and vanilla and stir. Press Sauté and once it bubbles, cook for 4 minutes, stirring often. Place the egg yolks into a bowl and whisk. Scoop up ½ cup (118ml) of the rice mixture and pour into the eggs and whisk well. Return the egg and rice mixture to the pot and stir. Cook for another 2 to 3 minutes, until the mixture thickens, stirring often. Carefully lift the inner pot out of the device and allow the mixture to cool and thicken, for about 30 minutes, stirring occasionally. Serve warm or cold. Add cinnamon to taste.

DAIRY, GLUTEN-FREE

HANDS-ON TIME: 6 Minutes

TIME TO PRESSURE: 5 Minutes

COOKING TIME: 12 Minutes on Rice function, 7 Minutes on Sauté function, plus 30 Minutes to sit and thicken

BUTTONS TO USE: Rice and Sauté

RELEASE TYPE: Full Natural Release, about 15 Minutes

ADVANCE PREP: May be made 2 days in advance

Serves 6–8

1 cup (185g) long grain rice, rinsed

1 cup (236ml) water

3½ cups (828ml) whole milk

⅔ cup (141g) light brown sugar

1 teaspoon pure vanilla extract

2 large egg yolks

ground cinnamon to taste

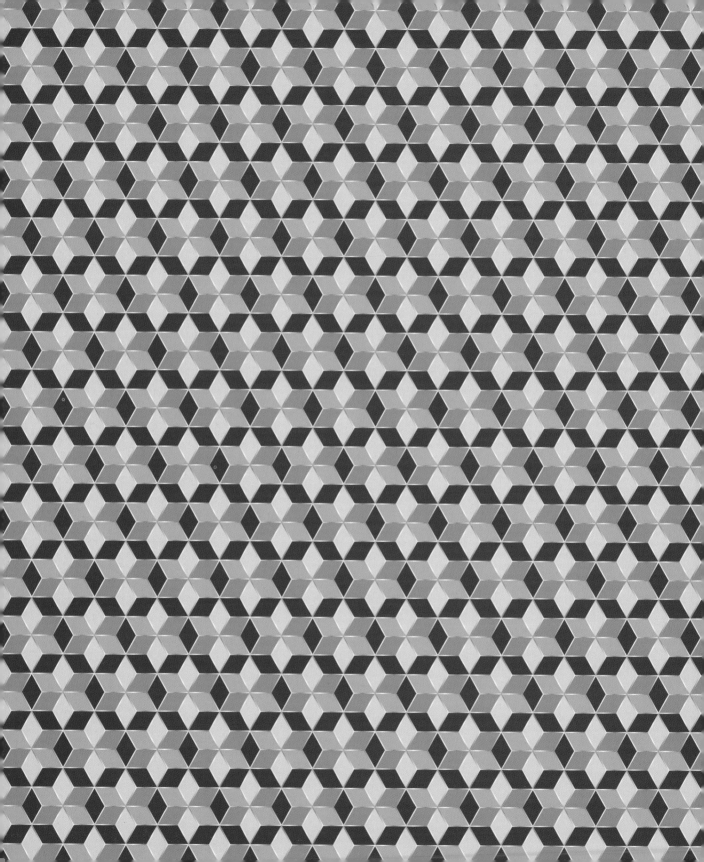

ABOUT THE AUTHOR

PAULA SHOYER, known as "The Kosher Baker," is the author of four prior cookbooks, her popular desserts in *The Kosher Baker* and *The Holiday Kosher Baker*, and her savory recipes in *The Healthy Jewish Kitchen* and *The New Passover Menu*.

Paula has been in the food business since 1995. She graduated with a pastry degree from the Ritz Escoffier in Paris, which inspired her to shift from practicing law and speechwriting first to catering and then teaching and writing. Paula does cooking and baking demonstrations and workshops all over the United States and even around the world, in places such as Canada, China, and Israel. She has taught teenagers to cook at summer camps for thirteen years and teaches private classes as well.

She is a freelance writer for several publications, including *The Washington Post*, *Jewish Food Experience*, *Hadassah Magazine*, *thekitchn*, *Whisk Magazine*, *Bnai Brith Magazine*, and more. She has judged several cooking competitions and been the emcee, and she is a busy public speaker on subjects such as her personal journey, how to take the calories out of Jewish comfort foods, the history of Jewish cookbooks, and how traditional Jewish foods become hip. She has served as a recipe editor for both traditionally published cookbooks and self-published family recipe compilations.

Paula competed on Food Network's *Sweet Genius* and has appeared on TV more than forty times, including in Israel. She is a regular guest on *Good Morning Washington* on WJLA and other Washington, D.C., stations. Paula has been on *Home and Family* multiple times, as well as *Fox News New York*, *San Diego Living*, and more.

In 2015 Paula was honored by Jewish Women International as a "Woman to Watch," and in 2016 as a "kosher food pioneer" by the Jewish Food Media Community.

We all need comfort food, especially these days, and no one really wants to give up favorite recipes, even if we know they are unhealthy for us. Paula takes cherished traditional Jewish food recipes and lightens them up while preserving the integrity of their taste and connection to family food history. She is also an expert at developing recipes for people with food allergies.

You can find Paula at www.thekosherbaker .com.

Paula is on Instagram as @kosherbaker and on Facebook as Paula Shoyer and The Kosher Baker. She created a Facebook group called Kosher Baker where others share their Jewish desserts.

Paula lives in Chevy Chase, Maryland, with her husband, who is always on a diet, and four hungry children.

ACKNOWLEDGMENTS

Thank you to my wonderful husband, Andy, and the best children ever: Emily, Sam, Jake, and Joey, who cheer me on always, and eat the food when they are around. I love you all.

To my team of cheerleaders:

My wonderful extended family: Ezra, Yonatan, Naomi, Adam, Steve, Debbie, Claire, and Ben.

Friends: Limor, Judith, Elena, Amanda, Wendy, Kathy, Lily, Pamela, Karina, Robyn, Tsila, Laurie, Marla, Susan, Andrea, Pam, Pam, Tammy, Aviva, Naomi, Chanie, Liz, and Esti. Thanks for all your support always.

Thanks to Betty Supo for all the kitchen help, but also for your expert advice when recipes fail. Gracias y besos.

I have great recipe testers for every book, but this time I had a very devoted and skilled group who were detailed in their comments and really helped me perfect these recipes. I am indebted to Melissa Arking, Sarah Feinberg, Trudy Jacobson, Barbara Libbin, Nicole Rosen, Dafna Sherman, Steve Shoyer, Edna Schrank, Lawrence LeVine, Ruthy Bodner, Bonnie Handel, Marsha Lefko, Lori Marcus, Elanit Jacobovics, and Katie Wexler.

Much gratitude to the dedicated and talented editing, design, and photography team: Hannah Reich, Heather Schlueter, Kimberly Broderick, Chris Bain, Jo Obarowski, Shannon Plunkett, David Ter-Avanesyan, and Bill Milne, our amazing photographer. To my chief editor, Jennifer Williams, thank you for being my biggest supporter and honoring my vision.

Thank you to my agent, Sally Ekus, of the Lisa Ekus Group. Thanks to Stuart Schnee and Trina Kaye, who have helped me share my message over the past several years.

INDEX

Note: Page numbers in *italics* indicate photos separate from recipes.

PHOTO CREDITS

Photography by Bill Milne, with the following exceptions:

Getty Images/iStock: AmaliaEka: 167; bhofack2: 99; JMRPhotography: 178; joannatkaczuk: 55; karisssa: 67; melissahelddesigns: throughout (graphics); joannatkaczuk: 55; mstahlphoto: 57

Paula Shoyer: 39, 63, 177

Shutterstock: AS Food Studio: 81; Christina: 105; dancewithwords: xiii; freeskyline: 140;

MariaKovaleva: 157; Ahanov Michael: 21; Oksana Mizina: 53; Irina Rostokina: 9; Slim79: x

StockFood: ©Leigh Beisch: 135; ©Maximilian Carlo Schmidt: 93; ©Jan-Peter Westerman: 119

Stocksy United: ©Cameron Whitman: 113